BIG BOOK of TOY AIRPLANES

identification & value guide

W. Tom Miller, Ph.D.

COLLECTOR BOOKS

A Division of Schroeder Publishing Co., Inc.

FRONT COVER:
Over the title: Hubley "Bremen" (cast iron), $1,000.00 – 1,500.00.
Under the title: Union Models GeeBee "Super R" racer, $30.00 – 50.00.
Center left: Nakajima McDonnell F-4 Phantom, $100.00 – 150.00.
Center right: Aeromini Boeing 727, $70.00 – 100.00.
Bottom left: Hubley Lockheed P-38, $150.00 – 200.00.
Bottom right: Hubley Curtiss P-40, $80.00 – 150.00.

BACK COVER:
Top: Lintoy Boeing 747 w/shuttle, $20.00 – 35.00.
Center left: ERTL Lockheed F-117, $20.00 – 35.00.
Center right: Tootsietoy DC-2, $75.00 – 125.00.
Bottom: Red Baron Biplane, $5.00 – 20.00.

Cover design by Beth Summers
Book design by Lisa Henderson
Photos by W. Tom Miller, Ph.D.

COLLECTOR BOOKS
P.O. Box 3009
Paducah, Kentucky 42002-3009

www.collectorbooks.com

Copyright © 2005 W. Tom Miller, Ph.D.

The current values in this book should be used only as a guide. They are not intended to set prices, which vary from one section of the country to another. Auction prices as well as dealer prices vary greatly and are affected by condition as well as demand. Neither the author nor the publisher assumes responsibility for any losses that might be incurred as a result of consulting this guide.

Searching For A Publisher?

We are always looking for people knowledgeable within their fields. If you feel that there is a real need for a book on your collectible subject and have a large comprehensive collection, contact Collector Books.

CONTENTS

DEDICATION

This book is dedicated to a good friend and toy dealer extraordinaire — the late Karlos Bader.

ACKNOWLEDGMENTS

The author would like to thank all those who have so generously helped in accumulating data and photos that have made this volume possible. I would like to give special thanks to Frank Kidd, Lysle Pickard, Dan Davis, Jim Thayer, Keith Schneider, and John Pierre for their assistance in finding toys that are included here. Also, I appreciate the input of G.R. Webster, Sy Merrall, Anthony Lawler, and others from the International Miniature Aircraft Collector's Society, and the knowledge gained from the Antique Toy Collectors of America regarding toy collecting and the history of toy manufacturing in the United States. Acknowledgment is made of the contribution by *Antique Toy World* editor Dale Kelley, and fellow airplane admirer John West (artist), whose humor is truly appreciated. Also, gratitude is directed to the writers whose articles on toy planes have been so stimulating and educational. Last but not least thanks to my wife Rowena for being understanding about the toy collection, and our children who learned over the years the difference between "children's toys" and "Dad's toys."

TOY PLANE COLLECTING

In recent years collecting toy planes has become popular with many who have been enthralled with aviation. For some of us involved with aviation over many years, collecting toy planes has been an on-going process. Some young people are starting collections because of occupations with airlines, military service, or other aviation involvement.

This book is intended for both the collector and the toy dealer to assist in identifying specific toy planes that are commonly found at collectible shops and toy shows. It is not totally complete of all the toy planes which have been built over time and that may be for sale today, but it will offer some guide to the extent of models which may be available and give an insight to the range of pricing which can be useful when buying toy planes.

The arrangement of this volume is based upon the main categories of toy planes, with listings in alphabetical order by manufacturer's name. This enables the collector to view some of the items from the line of products from each manufacturer, but of course the space available here does not allow us to illustrate all products available from each manufacturer. Nor do we have room to include some of the other firms who have also produced toy planes for the market.

The toy categories are based upon the type of material they are made from and/or the process by which they are fabricated. The variety of materials used include cast iron, lead, white metal, resin, tinplate, sheet steel, glass, and paper. The processes vary — sand molds for cast iron, elaborate and very expensive tooled dies for the detailed diecast models, dies used with stamping presses to shape pressed steel models, simple molds for casting low temperature metal alloys in slush casting, and different types of molds for molding resin models.

There are other categories of these miniature airplanes such as their functional use. Some have served as desk ornaments with others being ashtrays. Some are models of the real airplanes built for airlines or military forces and are displayed in the offices of airplane manufacturers. In the past large models were a marketing tool for travel agencies. The models were marked with airline markings and thus related to special travel programs featured by certain airlines. Other toy planes have been used as premiums in marketing programs as those linked with comic characters may have had a relationship to a product promotion with an entertainment or fast food company.

Published price guides are sometimes misleading with prices quoted being different than actual prices charged at sales and auctions. There is some differential between prices charged in various geographic areas of the United States, and variations which may exist for Canada and other countries. Also, dealers will charge prices based upon their cost and the value they place on the item, so expect prices to range fairly widely for identical items.

The price range listed in this volume is based upon a concensus of a group of collectors and dealers who frequent toy shows and survey auction catalogs. Also a record has been maintained for over 20 years of prices listed in published advertisements and reports of show and auction sales results. The pricing here is based upon the item being in good condition with no defects, original throughout mechanically, original paint, and no restoration. It is incumbent upon the seller to advise the customer if defects exist or repair has been undertaken on the model, particularly with the older antiques which become pricey and represent a substantial investment. Exceptional toys, such as mint with original box, have greater value than the toys alone, so save the toy's box if there is one. Also the toy that shows little wear may bring a premium over the price range listed.

The description of each toy plane listed here shows the model name, designator, wingspan, and the date of the toy's origin if known. This last factor is primarily to differentiate between the more valued toys that come from the 1920s, 1930s, and earlier, and those more recent mass-produced cheaper items that have flooded toy stores over the past thirty years. Symbols "N.A." used herein mean "not available" or "no answer."

Many older collectors have been model builders in the past, and the models of long ago made of balsa wood and Japanese tissue were fragile and did not last long, where the diecast, tin, and solid resin models have a shelf life that far exceeds those models of prior years. Frequently collectors select a single category of model aircraft that is favored, and while a few collect any or all types, it may be necessary to specialize or restrict a collection due to space, costs, or even spousal constraints.

Some collectors join clubs which bring together the collectors of particular brands of toys. The Dinky Club and the Matchbook Collectors Club are two examples that were organized to advise collectors of new toy releases and assist in promoting product sales. It was reported that in 1980 there were 750,000 members in the Matchbook Collectors Club — a sizeable number of collectors worldwide. They were all interested in these miniature toys, with probably most of them interested in the "wheel toys," the autos, tractors, and items which made up the early product line of the Matchbook Co. The airplanes came later to fill out the line. Dinky produced aircraft toys from as early as 1934, with a wide range of models in their line that continued until the late 1960s. This line extended from early propeller planes to modern fighter and airline jets. Their collector club dates back a number of years based on the catalog's announcement in 1994, although the number of members was not stated.

Another group interested in toy planes is the World Airline Historical Society, an international organization of aviation fans who collect airline memorablia. With diversified interests in collecting material about airlines, their collections range from photos, insignia, airline food utensils, airline schedules, and aircraft models with airline markings. They have periodic swap meets in the hub cities where collectors meet to buy and sell their different commodities.

To facilitate a flow of information about plane collectors and collections throughout the world, G.R. Webster formed an organization during the 1980s. The organization published an all-color newsletter "The Plane News," a quarterly, and featured illustrated articles on model planes and plane collections. This group sponsored swap meets in the U.S. on both the east and west coasts, and in Europe. Photos in "The Plane News" of member's miniature aircraft and descriptive comments gave readers an insight to the extent and nature of various collections. Also, certain collectors described how they would customize models according to their own collection criteria. The publication helped members identify models, establish the extent of product lines, and announce new items in the world market of miniature aircraft. The organization was known as the International Miniature Aircraft Collectors, a group with interests in diverse categories of miniature airplanes. (The organization is no longer active due to the founder's move to Europe.)

The beginning of my collection came about because my wood and plastic models were annihilated during our moves around the country. About 1970 I saw a new line of very detailed, diecast metal airplane toys with retracting landing gear and other moving parts. This line became my entry into toy plane collecting. Upon investigation I learned about other metal planes produced in the past and the collection began to grow. I found out that older toy planes were available in antique shops and at collectible shows. Then I met a man — Karlos Bader — who shared my enthusiasm for toy planes and was an antique toy dealer. He regularly toured all toy shows along the West Coast from San Diego to Vancouver, British Columbia, and his acquisitions from these shows were instrumental in enlarging my toy plane collection.

When I began collecting I was happy to find modestly priced desk models, cigarette lighters, ashtrays, small toys, and aero trinkets that did not tax my pocketbook, but offered some pleasure in being a replica of an aircraft I had photographed in the past. Then as the hobby became more addictive I found the pricing escalated for the items that held my interest and purchases became a major decision of whether or not to spend the amount for the item. A cast iron toy that became available at $1,000 was sold to another buyer before I could make a decision to purchase it. My hesitation cost me another $300 as I finally acquired it from the buyer.

Later my dealer friend told me he had the same toy five years earlier priced at only $100, and had it in inventory over a year, and ultimately sold it — but below his cost. The element of time and inflation affects cost, and the timing of the decision to purchase may influence the price you pay for an item. Those who began collecting in the 1950s were able to accumulate a collection when prices were a mere fraction of present values! Perhaps one should heed a suggestion made by other collectors that if you find an item you really want, buy it without hesitation if you can afford it.

My collection came to a point where there was no more display room available in my cabinets and I had to make a decision on how to restrict future acquisitions. Evaluating the inventory I decided to retain only diecast and cast iron toy planes, plus a few exceptions as examples of the many other categories of miniature aircraft available.

Some people collect desk/promotional models furnished by aircraft manufacturers to their best customers. Others acquire wind tunnel models used to test aircraft designs prior to production. Still others collect the large models made of either metal or resin that in years past would adorn travel agency offices to attract ticket buyers. These models were usually finely detailed and real attention-getters.

Some collectors specialized in the Japanese-built tin planes which were usually designed from specific models of airliners, military fighters, or bombers. Within this group there are wind-up toys and battery operated toys whose capability included flashing lights, rolling wheels, turning props, and, with some, even audio noise of revving motors.

Other collections are structured to include unpainted models so that the collector can replicate the colors of particular airlines or air force squadrons. The variety of collections extends afar with model sizes ranging from ½" in wingspan to over 12 feet. A cutaway jet transport model viewed in a passenger terminal showed all the

seating in a 747 airliner and this model had a wingspan of about 20 feet. (Dramatic to view, but unworkable for my collection.)

During World War II another type of aircraft model surfaced. Known as identification models, a variety of miniatures of U. S. and foreign aircraft were built to aid servicemen and civilians identify friend and foe aircraft types. Many of these sets of models were built in 1:72 scale (sometimes other scales as well) of such materials as metal, wood, or several forms of plastic. These sets permitted training in knowing the differences between an American P-51 fighter and a German ME-109 and British Spitfire. A number of major private collections of these I.D. models exist and duplicates are traded and sold frequently at collectible shows.

Several individuals have extensive collections that include toys and models built long ago, shortly after the beginning of manned flight. There are a number of replicas of Wright planes in model form built prior to W.W. I. Another early aircraft that has been modeled is the Bleriot of 1910. Some collections include both these models, which probably were acquired in Europe because France, Germany, and Britain saw more aviation activity between 1903 and 1910 than the U.S. (The Wright brothers received little recognition in the U.S. after their first few flights so they moved their demonstrations to France and spent several years creating interest abroad.) With the flight activity in Europe model planes appeared as toys for children and those that still remain in collections are highly desirable.

CAST IRON TOY PLANES

Cast iron toy planes, like cast iron toy autos, cast iron trains, and cast iron horse-drawn vehicles, are becoming rare. Products of another age, these toys are no longer made and since they date back 70 or more years, their life span has nearly reached the maximum one would expect from a child's toy. Those that do remain show their age unless their owner was a very caring child or had the unusual perception to recognize the potential value of the toy a half-century in the future.

Not long ago the Antique Toy Collectors of America had a convention in the Midwest where the program included visiting collectors' homes. Some of these collections had been started years ago and were unusually large. One collection of cast iron horse-drawn fire equipment was displayed on wall mounted shelves that stretched from near ceiling to floor in several rooms. One of the visitors was overheard to say "this is why you never see these at shows, nowadays. All that were ever made are here in this collection."

Nevertheless, one can still find a few cast iron planes at shows, and some will be advertised in collector trade magazines and auction catalogs. From the information available, cast iron toys had their beginning in America. Foundries began to appear in the mid 1600s in Europe, but it wasn't until the 1890s to 1900 that U.S. metal product manufacturers began to produce cast iron toys. Review of catalogs from the more prominent cast iron toy producers show a progression from banks, stoves, household novelties, then the wheel toys such as pull trains, fire wagons, police patrols, autos, and then finally airplanes.

As airplanes became more common and pioneering flights caught public attention, cast iron toy makers featured models that resembled the planes used in these historic flights. The 1928 Hubley catalog shows the cast iron "Lindy" glider and the New York to Paris Ryan monoplane used by Lindbergh on his solo flight across the Atlantic Ocean in 1927. Hubley also offered the largest cast iron toy plane made, the "America," a trimotor Fokker monoplane which Commander (later Admiral)

Richard Byrd used to cross the Atlantic, shortly after Lindbergh's solo flight. Hubley also produced several sizes of the German flying boat the DO-X which traversed the Atlantic in a ten month long trip to the U.S.A. during 1930 – 1931. Another product which found favor with the younger set was a toy iron Fokker monoplane the "Friendship," modeled after the plane flown by aviatrix Amelia Earhart in her first crossing of the Atlantic. The "Friendship" is unique as it is mounted on "floats" (cast iron) with wheels inserted in the floats so that the toy can be pulled along the floor by its youthful owner. The "Bremen," a German built airplane, was the first plane to fly the Atlantic Ocean east to west. Hubley built and sold replicas of the "Bremen" in two sizes celebrating this notable flight.

Although Hubley produced more cast iron toy plane models than any other manufacturer, several other cast iron toy producers were prominent in the toy market. Dent Hardware Co. of Fullerton, Pennsylvania; Arcade Manufacturing Co. of Freeport, Illinois; the A. C. Williams Co. of Ravenna, Ohio; and Vindex Toy Division of the National Sewing Machine Co. of Belvidere, Illinois, were also major producers of cast iron planes. Some of the factories made their planes from aluminum as well as cast iron and customers had a choice of materials within certain models. In the mid 1930s cast iron was virtually abandoned by the manufacturers in favor of diecast and slush cast metal products.

Catalogs for many manufacturers still exist in reproduction form. Curiosity about the origin of many of these toys motivated my research into when certain toys were first introduced to the market. As a result there are a number of catalogs and reprints of others in my files. While there are many gaps in years due to a lack of resources available, it is possible to identify production years of many toy planes within a reasonable range.

Among the many iron planes to be found there are a few which have confounded collectors regarding their origin. The iron monoplane with the imprint "Goodwill" on the top of its wing is considered to be named after the national air tour made by Charles Lindbergh following his New York to Paris flight. This toy has not been found in any of the cast iron catalogs seen, and one of the toy dealers who specializes in cast iron claims to have only known of two units in his years selling iron toys. Perhaps a late production change by altering the wing imprint or else a low production run was terminated due to some more important incident in aviation that involved a newer product.

Another cast iron toy plane whose origin is still a mystery is the "Bleriot" type monoplane with the letters "U.S." on the side of the fuselage. This type of plane was used by the U.S. Air Service in France for training U.S. pilots during World War I, and is pictured in *Colliers History of World War I* published in 1918. This type of plane has an origin in France, and the imprint "U.S." on the toy would provide the I.D. of the plane as being used by American forces. The Bleriot used for training in France was low powered and unable to fly, thus it was called the "Penquin." This does not afford us knowledge of who built the toy, whether the builder was an American firm, or when the toy arrived on the market. There are at least three or four of this model known to be in collections, and due to its design, the spool wheel is to wind a string around so that the plane becomes a pull-toy. (This may be the earliest of the iron toy planes.) These mysteries remain to be solved and the search continues for the origin of these rare birds.

Cast iron is long gone but some of these toys have endured the better part of a century. Now we must be satisfied with cast metal toys that have great detail but are more expensive. (In 1932 the Vindex cast iron Lockheed Air Express was priced at $7.20 per dozen, while now it is valued at about $5,000.) Foundries have all but disappeared with the exception of those still producing furnace and farm implement parts.

The cast iron toys that remain today should be enshrined to mark an era in America's industrial progress and to demonstrate the virtue of durability of iron toys compared to the fragility of today's plastics. There is a certain amount of romance in these hunks of iron that speaks of aviation itself from the same period of time, when rugged beauty in aircraft design prevailed. (Ford's "Tin Goose," the rugged Fokker tri-motors, "Bremen" and its corrugated dural skin, heavy Liberty motors, Martin biplane bombers, and other examples that differ so radically from today's aerodynamic designs.) Today, iron toy planes are definitely art objects, not just old toys!

Arcade Mfg. Co., Freeport, Illinois

Started as an industrial foundry in 1869, the Novelty Iron and Brass Foundry produced castings for commercial use. Restructured about 1885, it took the name Arcade Mfg. Co. Their 1934 catalog shows the Ford trimotor toy plus numerous auto toys, and a variety of other products ranging from lawnmowers to Christmas tree holders.

Model:	Vultee "Valiant" BT-13
Year:	1940
Wingspan:	10"
Price Range:	$350.00 – 400.00

This W.W.II Vultee trainer is made up with a cast iron fuselage and a sheet steel wing. The landing gear struts are sheet steel and the wheels are made of wood.

Model:	Monocoupe
Year:	1930s
Wingspan:	4"
Price Range:	$225.00 – 275.00

This iron replica of the Monocoupe has nickel-plated wheels and propeller.

Model:	Boeing 247
Year:	1930s
Wingspan:	4"
Price Range:	$100.00 – 150.00

This Boeing 247 transport model is cast iron with nickel plating and has the name "Boeing" cast into the top of the wing.

Model:	Monocoupe 90
Year:	1930s
Wingspan:	8½"
Price Range:	$750.00 – 950.00

This is the middle-size Monocoupe in the Arcade line, exceeded by only the model with an 11" wing. This toy was modified by a former youthful owner by the addition of an engine drag ring similar to ones used on the original planes.

Model:	Ford Trimotor
Year:	1930s
Wingspan:	4"
Price Range:	$100.00 – 150.00

A two-piece iron replica of the 1925 Ford transport has rubber wheels and sheet steel propellers.

Dent Hardware Co., Fullerton, Pennsylvania

The Dent Hardware Co. began operations in 1895 and continued until 1973. Their auto toys were equipped with rubber tires and they produced boxed sets of toys including an airport set shown in the 1928 catalog. The company also advertised a 6" dirigible and 6" "Lucky Boy" glider, both of which retailed for twenty five cents each. Another featured plane was an aluminum cast Ford trimotor in several sizes with the largest having a 10" wingspan and retailing for $1.00 each.

Model:	"Lucky Boy" monoplane
Year:	1929
Wingspan:	10"
Price Range:	$1,500.00 – 2,000.00

This monoplane is a three-piece iron casting with the wing and two side pieces of the fuselage making up the basic parts. The words "Lucky Boy" and stars in a circle are molded in raised relief on the top of the wing. It has rubber tires, a wooden tail wheel, and a nickel-plated propeller.

Model:	"Lucky Boy" monoplane
Year:	1930s
Wingspan:	4"
Price Range:	$300.00 – 350.00

This plane dates to years just following Lindbergh's "lucky" flight from New York to Paris. Stars in circles are in raised relief on top of the wing and the plane has nickel-plated wheels and engine.

Model:	"Goodwill" monoplane
Year:	1930s
Wingspan:	4¾"
Price Range:	$1,800.00 – 2,500.00

A rare iron monoplane, it has a nickel-plated engine, landing gear, wheels, and prop. The words "Goodwill" and stars in circles are raised on top of the wing. This toy is modeled after Lindbergh's Ryan New York to Paris plane with which he toured many American cities following his Paris flight.

Model:	"Air Express" – Fokker trimotor
Year:	1929
Wingspan:	12½"
Price Range:	$5,000.00 – 7,000.00

A durable iron toy, the "Air Express" name and stars in circles are molded into the top of the wing. The rudder has numbers "NX4474" molded on both sides, and props are nickel plated. This plane is fairly rare in the toy market.

Model:	Ford trimotor
Year:	1930
Wingspan:	12"
Price Range:	$1,500.00 – 2,500.00

Molded in aluminum, the corrugations in the casting replicate the corrugated metal covering of the real Ford trimotor.

Hubley Manufacturing Co., Lancaster, Pennsylvania

Hubley has been the most prominent of toy airplane manufacturers with an early start into cast iron models as aviation began, and continued into diecast and pressed steel models beyond the 1940s. Their beginning in 1892 was with solely cast iron products and toy planes are featured in the 1928, 1929, and 1932 catalogs. As notable flights were made by Lindbergh, Amelia Earhart, and others, Hubley produced toys which were a good likeness of their airplanes and these became popular with children and later highly desired collectibles.

Model:	"America" – Fokker trimotor
Year:	1928
Wingspan:	17"
Price Range:	$7,000.00 – 10,000.00

Largest of all the cast iron toy planes, the "America" has its name in raised letters across the top wing and twin pilots sit in the open cockpit. As the plane is pulled along the floor, propellers turn by means of cables linked to the wheels. The America was flown non-stop across the Atlantic Ocean by Richard (Adml.) Byrd in 1927.

Model:	Four-engine transport
Year:	1936
Wingspan:	5½"
Price Range:	$350.00 – 500.00

This transport plane has twin rudders and the propellers are nickel plated. This is one of few aircraft toys that does not resemble a specific plane.

Model:	Low-wing monoplane
Year:	1930s
Wingspan:	5"
Price Range:	$100.00 – 150.00

This toy has nickel-plated wings and oversize rubber tires and resembles numerous low wing aircraft in use during the 1930s. This model was available in assorted colors.

Model:	Low wing monoplane
Year:	1930s
Wingspan:	3¾"
Price Range:	$75.00 – 100.00

Model;	"Bremen" – Junkers monoplane
Year:	1929
Wingspan:	10"
Price Range:	$5,000.00 – 8,000.00

The large rare "Bremen" is distinguished by wingtips turned up and markings "Junkers Bremen" on the body and the numbers "D1167" on the wing all in raised relief. The tail wheel uses a rubber tire and the two main wheels are nickel plated. The "Bremen" was the first plane to cross the Atlantic from Dublin, Ireland, to Labrador. The pilot and passengers are visible in the cabin.

Model:	"Bremen" – Junkers monoplane
Year:	1930s
Wingspan:	6½"
Price Range:	$1,000.00 – 1,500.00

Model:	Ryan NY-P
Year:	1928
Wingspan:	13½"
Price Range:	$3,500.00 – 4,500.00

Largest of the "Lindy" models, this toy has details of the original plane with realistic wing struts, NY-P decals, and the Ryan's number, "NX211," marked on the rudder. The name "Lindy" is in raised relief on top of the wing and "Ryan NY-P" is on the rudder. As the wheels roll, the attached cable turns the prop.

Model:	"Lindy" monoplane
Year:	1928
Wingspan:	3½"
Price Range:	$125.00 – 250.00

One of several smaller size "Lindy" models produced by Hubley Co.

Model:	Douglas DC-3
Year:	1938
Wingspan:	5⅝"
Price Range:	$250.00 – 350.00

This toy models the DC-3 which first flew in 1935. The wings and props are nickel plated and the markings "TAT" and "NC-431" are raised on the top of the wings.

Model:	Dornier Do X flying boat
Year:	1930s
Wingspan:	8"
Price Range:	$4,000.00 – 5,000.00

Largest of the Do X models, this iron toy has rubber tires and nickel-plated engines above the top wing.

Model:	Dornier Do X flying boat
Year:	1929
Wingspan:	4"
Price Range:	$350.00 – 450.00

Model:	Lockheed "Sirius"
Year:	1932
Wingspan:	10½"
Price Range:	$7,000.00 – 9,000.00

This rare toy was modeled after the plane used by Charles Lindbergh and his wife Anne as they surveyed Pacific airline routes for Pan Am Airlines in 1931. Equipped with pilots in the cockpits, nickel prop, and Lindy's name on the wing, this toy plane is seldom seen except at toy auctions.

Model:	Air Ford
Year:	1928
Wingspan:	3¾"
Price Range:	$75.00 – 125.00

This toy was modeled after the Ford "Flivver" of 1926. The small sport plane was unsuccessful in the marketplace, but Hubley sold many of the toys. The real plane is displayed at the Ford Museum in Dearborn, Michigan.

Model:	Gyro plane
Year:	1929
Wingspan:	3¾"
Price Range:	$150.00 – 250.00

Modeled after the Pitcarin Autogiro, this toy has nickel-plated rotors, propeller, and wheels. The name "Gyro plane" is in raised relief on top of the wing.

Model:	Fokker F-7 "Friendship" trimotor floatplane
Year:	1929
Wingspan;	13"
Price Range:	$3,500.00 – 5,000.00

This pull toy is modeled after the Fokker transport made in the U.S. and used by Amelia Earhart in her non-stop flight over the Atlantic in 1928. With wheels mounted in the floats, the toy may be pulled along the floor. The name "Friendship" is in raised relief on the wing.

Kenton Hardware Mfg. Co., Kenton, Ohio

Begun in 1890, Kenton made iron toy horse carts, autos, and later planes. Toy autos dominated production until operations ceased in 1952.

Model:	"Air Mail" monoplane
Year:	1932
Wingspan:	5½"
Price Range:	$350.00 – 450.00

This iron monolane is typical of the 1932 monoplanes such as the Stinson SM8A, the Ryan Brougham, and others used for private and commercial flying. This toy has "Air Mail" in raised relief on the wing and metal wheels.

Model:	"Pony Blimp"
Year:	1930s
Length:	6"
Price Range:	$250.00 – 350.00

Blimps and dirigibles were popular children's toys in this era, and many types and sizes of such toys were offered by toy stores.

Kilgore Mfg. Co., Westerville, Ohio

Kilgore Co. initiated operations about 1925 and produced several models of cast iron toy planes. It has been reported their primary products were cap pistols which were made until the company was disbanded in the 1940s.

Model:	Travelair "Mystery" ship
Year:	1930s
Wingspan:	7"
Price Range:	$600.00 – 900.00

The Travelair Mystery ship shocked U.S. aviation at the 1929 National Air Races with its speed which exceeded even the military planes. The toy has its name in relief on the wing, and has nickel wheels, engine, and prop. A variant model used a separate one-piece wing which was bolted to the fuselage ahead of the cockpits.

Model:	"Bullet"
Year:	1930s
Wingspan:	4"
Price Range:	$125.00 – 175.00

This open cockpit toy has its name in relief on the wing.

Model:	"Super Seagull"
Year:	1930s
Wingspan:	8½"
Price Range:	$1,800.00 – 2,500.00

This model is a rarity at toy shows due to very limited production when manufactured in the 1930s.

Model:	"Seagull"
Year:	1930s
Wingspan:	8"
Price Range:	$1,000.00 – 1,500.00

This flying boat toy resembles the Fokker F-11 which was used for private and commercial flying in the 1930s. "Sea Gull" is in relief on the wing, and the three wheels, engine, and prop are all nickel plated.

Model:	Ford trimotor
Year:	1930s
Wingspan:	13½"
Price Range:	$4,000.00 – 5,000.00

This Ford trimotor is one of the most realistic cast iron toys produced. It is a historic model because of the Ford's role in initiating transcontinental flight across the U.S. The casting simulates the corrugated skin of the Ford plane and the airline's initials "T.A.T" are cast onto the side of the body. Nickel-plated wheels, engines, and props are used.

Vindex Toys and Novelties, Belvidere, Illinois

A division of National Sewing Machine Co., Vindex Toys had a short run in operations during the worst of the Depression. The firm lasted less than five years.

Model:	"Air Express"
Year:	1932
Wingspan:	9¾"
Price Range:	$4,000.00 – 5,000.00

This toy is modeled after the Lockheed Air Express which was one of the fastest planes in the sky during this era. The name "Lockheed" is molded in the top of the wing and a nickel-plated prop, engine cowling, and wheels are used. Vindex models are rare to toy sales but occasionally show up at toy auctions. The Vindex catalog of 1932 quotes a price for this model of $14.00 a dozen, but shows a price revision that reduces the price by 50%.

A. C. Williams Co., Ravenna, Ohio

Established in 1886 the Williams company produced wagon wheels, axles, and other products in their foundry operaton. As time moved on sales for their products declined and they turned to toy products such as autos, wagons, and planes. The firm continued through W.W.II, but converted to industrial casting products.

Model:	UX-166 monoplane
Year:	1930s
Wingspan:	6"
Price Range:	$250.00 – 300.00

This twin, open cockpit plane has its designator "UX166" in raised relief on top of the wing. There are also two stars in circles, and the engine and landing gear struts (a single casting) as well as the engine, prop, and wheels are nickel plated.

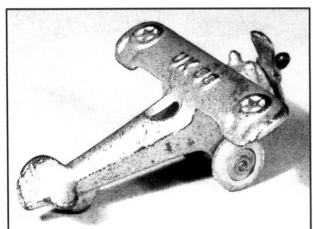

Model:	OXOO Monoplane
Year:	1930s
Wingspan:	3"
Price Range:	$150.00 – 200.00

This small iron toy has a single open cockpit, a plated prop, and rubber tires.

Unknown Origin

Model:	Bleriot trainer
Year:	N.A.
Wingspan:	6"
Price Range:	$2,500.00 – 4,000.00

A mystery toy that possibly dates back to World War I. The plane includes a pilot and the castings form an open frame fuse-lage and a wing with a pattern indicating a series of ribs. It has a spool undercarriage, presumably to wind a cord onto for means of pulling the toy along the floor. Reference material suggests this models a U.S. pilot trainer used in France in 1917 – 1918.

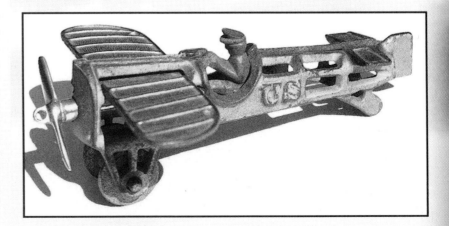

DIECAST TOY PLANES

Production of die cast planes began as early as the mid-1920s, reaching a peak in the late 1970s. There are a number of methods for casting metal and they range from simple molds as used in slush casting to the expensive, finely machined dies used to produce detailed models. As the need for mass production was stimulated by market demand, the processes that offered production economy were selected.

Early manufacturers such as Barclay, Kansas Toy & Novelty, Charles A. Woods, and Midgetoy produced "slush-cast" toys, while later manufacturers such as Aero-mini, Dinky, Edison Giocatelloi, Corgi, and Tekno used machine tooled dies and pressure casting to achieve the desired detailing on their models. This latter process requires considerable engineering applied to the model in order to cast the various parts such as landing gear, flaps, wheels, airstairs, and other minute parts that actually operate in some of these models.

The manufacturers in the Far East have built many different toy plane models which have been found in the toy stores and dime stores. Many brands from Asia have not endured for very long, and the products themselves have had a relatively short life. There have been many different airplane models built, but many of the firms in the market do not mark the items except for the term indicating the place of origin — "made in Hong Kong." These toys are on the low end of the pricing spectrum and usually retail in the U.S. for a dollar or less.

Some cast planes are unique. The cast aluminum Spirit of St. Louis is apparently the only toy built by Aluminum Industries, a precision casting firm located in Ohio. Research shows this company wrote a textbook on casting technique, but there is no evidence left to suggest their motivation for building this one toy. Only three years ago a firm in Toyko, Japan, introduced a beautiful model of the Gee Bee Super R racer which was briefly marketed in the U.S. Now the toy cannot be re-ordered by dealers because no trace remains of the company.

The three aluminum biplanes are precision built with metal struts fitted into the wings. No one seems to know who built these, or the reason they were made. Rumor among toy plane collectors was they were developed for a bid proposal by a firm interested in a contract to build I.D. models for the U.S. government just prior to W.W.II. Contact with a firm whose name had been mentioned as a possibility denied it had been their product, and no duplicates have been found since 1975.

The diecast models of interest follow here in alphabetical order of manufacturers, with those of unknown origin at the end of this section.

Parade Magazine, *October 21, 1990.*

Aeromini Inc., Farmingdale, New York

Aeromini designed and built some of the most detailed miniature planes that have been produced. All-metal toys, these planes were built in Japan and marketed for a few years in the 1970s.

Model:	Boeing 707
Year:	1970s
Wingspan:	7"
Price Range:	$75.00 – 150.00

This 707 has retractible landing gear.

Model:	Boeing 727
Year:	1970s
Wingspan:	5½"
Price Range:	$70.00 – 100.00

The 727 has retractible landing gear and an operating airstair.

Model:	Boeing 737
Year:	1970s
Wingspan:	5"
Price Range:	$45.00 – 100.00

The 737 has retractible landing gear.

Model:	Boeing 747
Year:	1970s
Wingspan:	8¼"
Price Range:	$200.00 – 250.00

This finely detailed model has a complex retractible landing gear.

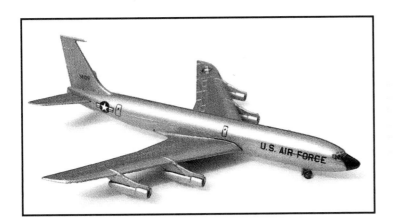

Model:	Boeing EC-135
Year:	1970s
Wingspan:	7"
Price Range:	$200.00 – 250.00

Model:	747 "Spirit of '76"
Year:	1970s
Wingspan:	8¼"
Price Range:	$300.00 – 350.00

Special markings similar to "Air Force One," and U.S. Bicentennial markings on the tail are on this 747.

Model:	Douglas DC-8
Year:	1970s
Wingspan:	7"
Price Range:	$175.00 – 250.00

This stretched version of the DC-8 has retractible landing gear.

Model:	Douglas DC-9
Year:	1970s
Wingspan:	4¾"
Price Range:	$70.00 – 100.00

The DC-9 has retractible landing gear and an operating airstair at the rear of the fuselage.

Model:	B.A.C. VC-10
Year:	1970s
Wingspan:	7"
Price Range:	$200.00 – 250.00

This jet transport has retractible landing gear.

Model:	McDonnell F-4 "Phantom" II
Year:	1970s
Wingspan:	4¾"
Price Range:	$250.00 – 350.00

The Phantom F-4 models have retractible landing gear.

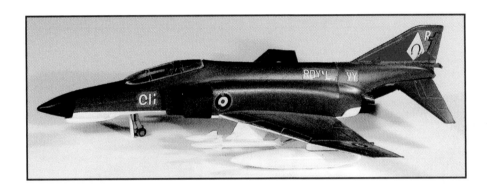

Model:	McDonnell F-4 "Phantom" (RNAF)
Year:	1970s
Wingspan:	4¾"
Price Range:	$250.00 – 300.00

Model:	Lockheed F-104
Year:	1970s
Wingspan:	3¼"
Price Range:	$200.00 – 250.00

The F-104 has retractible landing gear and a cockpit canopy that opens.

Model:	Mitsubishi "Zero"
Year:	1970s
Wingspan:	5¾"
Price Range:	$150.00 – 250.00

Aluminum Industries, Cincinnati, Ohio

Model:	Ryan Spirit of St. Louis
Year:	1928
Wingspan:	10½"
Price Range:	$250.00 – 500.00

This replica of Lindbergh's Spirit of St. Louis was the only toy made by this firm. The company had a reputation for expertise in precision casting but did not survive the Great Depression.

Avon Inc.

Model:	Wright "Flyer"
Year:	N.A.
Wingspan:	4"
Price Range:	$15.00 – 25.00

Barclay Mfg. Co., Hoboken, New Jersey (1924 – 1971)

Barclay toys were found in dime stores in the 1930s. and usually sold for only a nickel or a dime.

Model:	Lockheed "Vega"
Year:	1930s
Wingspan:	4"
Price Range:	$50.00 – 100.00

This toy resembles the "Vega" which had a round plywood body with the wood sheets bonded together for structural integrity. This toy has a tin wing fastened to the cast body.

Model:	Lockheed "Orion"
Year:	1930s
Wingspan:	3¾"
Price Range:	$35.00 – 60.00

This toy is marked with "U.S. Army" on the top of the wing.

Model:	Monoplane
Year:	1930s
Wingspan:	2¼"
Price Range:	$35.00 – 65.00

Buddy L Inc., Glen Falls, New York

Model:	Gee Bee racer
Year:	N.A.
Wingspan:	3½"
Price Range:	$20.00 – 40.00

Campo Co., Russia

Model:	Chica I-53
Year:	N.A.
Wingspan:	5¾"
Price Range:	$50.00 – 125.00

A design that dates back to Spain's war in the 1930s, this biplane toy has fine detail including a swiveling tailwheel and a movable rudder.

Model:	Ilushin "Stormovik" IL-2
Year:	N.A.
Wingspan:	8"
Price Range:	$50.00 – 125.00

One of the first-line fighters of the Russian Air Force in W.W.II, this model is an accurate replica in miniature of the real airplane.

Model:	MBR-2 seaplane
Year:	N.A.
Wingspan:	10"
Price Range:	$150.00 – 200.00

The MBR-2 saw service in the Baltic and Black Sea areas during W.W.II as reconnaissance seaplanes. Gun mounts are in the nose and rear turret.

Model:	Ilushin "Rata" I-16
Year:	N.A.
Wingspan:	5"
Price Range:	$50.00 – 125.00

Model:	MIG-15
Year:	N.A.
Wingspan:	5½"
Price Range:	$75.00 – 150.00

The MIG-15 was the counterpart of America's Sabrejet during the Korean conflict. This model shows great details of the real plane.

Model:	YAK –3
Year:	N.A.
Wingspan:	5"
Price Range:	$50.00 – 125.00

Model:	Lavochkin LA-5
Year:	N.A.
Wingspan:	5¼"
Price Range:	$50.00 – 125.00

Corgi-Mettoy Playcraft, Northampton, U.K.

Model:	"Aerocar"
Year:	1980
Wingspan:	6½"
Price Range:	$100.00 – 150.00

Similar to Molt Taylor's Aerocar design, this metal and plastic toy features an auto which can be detached from the wings and tail.

Model:	Lockheed "Constellation"
Year:	1998
Wingspan:	10"
Price Range:	$150.00 – 250.00

One of the top metal models of all time, this "Connie" is strikingly accurate in detail and markings.

Model:	"Concorde" SST
Year:	1979
Wingspan:	3¼"
Price range:	$20.00 – 35.00

The one success story of the supersonic transport age, the Concorde provided British Airways and Air France airlines with over a quarter century of airline service in a regime of supersonic flight for premium fare.

Model:	"Nipper" Mk. II
Year:	N.A.
Wingspan:	5"
Price Range:	$20.00 – 35.00

Model:	Lancaster transport
Year:	1998
Wingspan:	8½"
Price Range:	$75.00 – 125.00

C.I.J. Co. (Compagnie Industrielle du Jouet), Paris, France

The C.I.J. toy planes are cast in a heavy metal and have a nice paint finish that gives them a superior look to most of the cast toy planes.

Model:	Boeing 707
Year:	1970s
Wingspan:	5¼"
Price Range:	$30.00 – 65.00

Model:	Sud "Caravelle" SE 210
Year:	1970s
Wingspan:	4½"
Price Range:	$30.00 – 65.00

Danbury Mint, Norwalk, Connecticut

The Danbury Mint models are cast in pewter. With considerable detail, the models are elegant appearing and make a striking display in a trophy case. They are not toys to play with, but as a collector once expressed, "looking at the model of the real thing, gives you the feeling of pleasure that you get when you do view the real thing." A rather inane statement, but then collectors have unique ways of expressing what is pleasurable. The models ordered were sent to collectors over a period of time, rather than all being available for delivery at any one time.

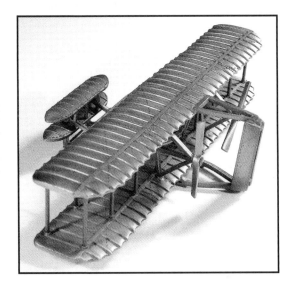

Model:	Wright "Flyer"
Year:	1983
Wingspan:	7"
Price Range:	$50.00 – 100.00

Model:	Ryan NY-P
Year:	1983
Wingspan:	8"
Price Range:	$50.00 – 75.00

Model:	Sopwith "Camel"
Year:	1983
Wingspan:	6½"
Price Range:	$100.00 – 135.00

Model:	Grumman "Hellcat"
Year:	1983
Wingspan:	5"
Price Range:	$50.00 – 75.00

Model:	Boeing B-17
Year:	1983
Wingspan:	8"
Price Range:	$50.00 – 100.00

Model:	Boeing 707
Year:	1983
Wingspan:	7"
Price Range:	$50.00 – 75.00

Model:	Douglas DC-3
Year:	1983
Wingspan:	7"
Price Range:	$50.00 – 75.00

Model:	Piper "Cub"
Year:	1983
Wingspan:	6½"
Price Range:	$50.00 – 75.00

Model:	NASA Space Shuttle
Year:	1983
Wingspan:	3"
Price Range:	$50.00 – 75.00

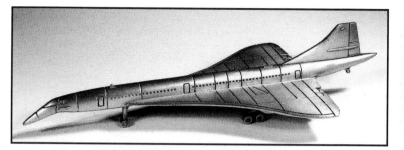

Model:	"Concorde" SST
Year:	1983
Wingspan:	3½"
Price Range:	$50.00 – 75.00

Model:	McDonnell-Douglas F-15 "Eagle"
Year:	1983
Wingspan:	4"
Price Range:	$50.00 – 75.00

Model:	Lockheed P-38
Year:	1983
Wingspan:	7"
Price Range:	$50.00 – 100.00

Model:	Sikorsky S-42 flying boat
Year:	1983
Wingspan:	7"
Price Range:	$100.00 – 150.00

Dinky (Meccano Ltd.), Great Britain

Evolving from the Hornby firm and their miniature railroad equipment, Meccano Miniatures began producing toy trains, motor vehicles, and farm animals in 1933. In 1934 Dinky Toys produced six airplanes to begin a long line of airplane toys that carried through until 1979 when they closed their doors. Through 45 years of production Dinky built about 75 models relating to the aviation and space programs.

Model:	"Singapore" flying boat
Year:	1936
Wingspan:	5"
Price Range:	$300.00 – 450.00

Modeled after a 1926 flying boat produced in Britain, this cast toy is easily identified by the double engines mounted between the wings.

Model:	Percival "Gull"
Year:	1936
Wingspan:	3"
Price Range:	$80.00 – 120.00

The "Gull" was made famous by aviatrix Jean Batten who flew her "Gull" from England to New Zealand in 1935.

Model:	Junkers JU-90
Year:	1938
Wingspan:	6¼"
Price Range:	$175.00 – 225.00

Scaled after a German airliner, the JU-90 carried 40 passengers at a speed of 250 mph.

Model:	Armstrong Whitworth "Ensign"
Year:	1938
Wingspan:	7"
Price Range:	$175.00 – 225.00

The "Ensign" was first of a fleet of four-engine transports placed in service with Imperial Airways in 1938.

Model:	Empire flying boat
Year:	1939
Wingspan:	6"
Price Range:	$250.00 – 300.00

A four-engine flying boat that was the base carrier for the Mayo composite set that included the Mercury seaplane, was intended to enable the Mercury to fly off the larger plane for cross-Atlantic flights.

Model:	Vickers "Jockey"
Year:	1934
Wingspan:	3"
Price Range:	$175.00 – 250.00

Model:	deHavilland "Albatross"
Year:	1939
Wingspan:	5"
Price Range:	$150.00 – 200.00

Model:	deHavilland "Comet I"
Year:	1935
Wingspan:	3½"
Price Range:	$200.00 – 250.00

This "Comet" racer was built for the 1934 England to Australia race and Scott & Black's entry won the race for England.

Model:	Sikorsky S-42 flying boat
Year:	1938
Wingspan:	6"
Price Range:	$200.00 – 250.00

The S-42 inaugurated over-water passenger service for both the Atlantic and Pacific oceans in 1935.

Model:	Boeing B-17
Year:	1939
Wingspan:	5½"
Price Range:	$150.00 – 250.00

Model:	Junkers "Stuka"
Year:	1969
Wingspan:	7½"
P rice Range:	$100.00 – 150.00

The "Stuka" dive-bomber was one of the Nazi top weapons as their forces invaded Poland and other territories at the start of W.W.II.

Model:	Short "Mercury" seaplane
Year:	1939
Wingspan:	4"
Price Range:	$75.00 – 125.00

Model:	Avro "Vulcan" bomber
Year:	1955
Wingspan:	6¼"
Price Range:	$2,000.00 – 5,000.00

A rare item, this toy was built of aluminum rather than the usual metal, and due to the high temperature the dies did not last beyond the initial low quantity run. Reports say those few models built were shipped to Canada and the U.S. for sale.

Model:	Hawker Siddeley 125
Year:	1970
Wingspan:	5½"
Price Range:	$75.00 – 100.00

Model:	McDonnell F-4 "Phantom"
Year:	1972
Wingspan:	5½"
Price Range:	$100.00 – 150.00

The F-4 "Phantom" became a mainstay of military air forces around the world. The prime fighter of U.S. military services, the F-4 was exported to many of the Allied countries during the 1970s.

Model:	Hawker "Harrier"
Year:	1970
Wingspan:	4½"
Price Range:	$100.00 – 150.00

The "Harrier," developed in England by Hawker, used fans for its vertical lift and "hover" capability in flight. Deemed a success, it was adopted by the U.S. Air Force and other military services.

Model:	S.E.P.E.C.A.T. "Jaguar"
Year:	1973
Wingspan:	4¼"
Price Range:	$75.00 – 100.00

Model:	Dassault "Mystere"
Year:	1959
Wingspan:	2½"
Price Range:	$35.00 – 50.00

Model:	Sud "Vatour"
Year:	1959
Wingspan:	3¼"
Price Range:	$40.00 – 60.00

Model:	Lockheed "Constellation"
Year:	1959
Wingspan:	8"
Price Range:	$200.00 – 300.00

Model:	Vickers "Viscount"
Year:	1956
Wingspan:	6"
Price Range:	$75.00 – 100.00

The "Viscount" turboprop transport was used by a number of airlines around the world. An early entry into turbo-power in the U.S., the "Viscount" was produced in a quantity of several hundred and served with over 30 airlines.

Model:	Beech "Baron"
Year:	1968
Wingspan:	5½"
Price Range:	$40.00 – 75.00

The "Baron" is a popular light-twin and is used for pleasure flying and most frequently as a corporate business aircraft.

Model:	Beech "Bonanza"
Year:	1965
Wingspan:	5¼"
Price Range:	$40.00 – 75.00

Introduced just after W.W.II, the "Bonanza" became a favorite of private flyers and it remained in production for decades. The "V-tail" was the feature that identified the Bonanza from other aircraft.

Model:	Lockheed P-80
Year:	1947
Wingspan:	2¼"
Price Range:	$30.00 – 50.00

Model:	Gloster "Javelin"
Year:	1956
Wingspan:	3¼"
Price Range:	$40.00 – 60.00

Model:	deHavilland "Sea Vixen"
Year:	1960
Wingspan:	3¼"
Price Range:	$40.00 – 60.00

Model:	English Electric "Lightning"
Year:	1959
Wingspan:	2¼"
Price Range:	$30.00 – 50.00

Model	Supermarine "Spitfire"
Year:	1945
Wingspan:	6¾"
Price Range:	$100.00 – 150.00

The "Spitfire" was one of the principal reasons the Nazi "blitzkrieg" was unsuccessful in invading England during W.W.II. Fighting off Luftwaffe air strikes, the "Spitfire" had air superiority in early stages of the war.

Model:	Supermarine "Spitfire" Mk.II
Year:	1979
Wingspan:	7"
Price Range:	$175.00 – 250.00

This chromed "Spitfire" was produced for the Diamond Jubilee of the Royal Air Force in 1979.

Model:	Hawker "Hurricane"
Year:	1972
Wingspan:	7½"
Price Range:	$150.00 – 200.00

The "Hurricane" teamed with the "Spitfire" in the Battle of Britain to withstand the aerial attacks on England and keep Germany from invading.

Model:	Messerschmidt BF-109
Year:	1972
Wingspan:	6½"
Price Range:	$125.00 – 200.00

The BF-109 was Germany's top fighter plane throughout W.W.II in Europe. Fast and maneuverable, the BF-109 had many victories.

Model:	Republic P-47 "Thunderbolt"
Year:	1975
Wingspan:	7½"
Price Range:	$150.00 – 250.00

This model of the P-47 is a shining example of a few toys that have a true, detailed look of the real airplane.

Model:	Mitsubishi "Zero"
Year:	1975
Wingspan:	7¼"
Price Range:	$150.00 – 200.00

Japan's "Zero" had an imposing battle record in W.W.II, and this model of the "Zero" is detailed and realistic.

Model:	Avro "York"
Year:	1946
Wingspan:	6¼"
Price Range:	$70.00 – 100.00

Model:	Gloster "Meteor"
Year:	1946
Wingspan:	2½"
Price Range:	$30.00 – 50.00

Model:	Supermarine "Swift"
Year:	1955
Wingspan:	2"
Price Range:	$30.00 – 50.00

Model:	Boeing 737
Year:	1970
Wingspan:	6"
Price Range:	$75.00 – 100.00

Model:	Hawker "Hunter"
Year:	1955
Wingspan:	2"
Price Range:	$30.00 – 50.00

Model:	deHavilland "Comet" airliner
Year:	1954
Wingspan:	7¼"
Price Range:	$75.00 – 100.00

Model:	Sud "Caravelle"
Year:	1962
Wingspan:	7¼"
Price Range:	$75.00 – 100.00

Model:	Bristol "Britannia"
Year:	1959
Wingspan:	9"
Price Range:	$200.00 – 300.00

Model:	Multi-role Combat Aircraft
Year:	1974
Wingspan:	6½"
Price Range:	$75.00 – 125.00

Model:	Armstrong Whitworth "Whitley"
Year:	1937
Wingspan:	4¾"
Price Range:	$200.00 – 250.00

Model:	Airspeed "Envoy"
Year:	1938
Wingspan:	4"
Price Range:	$225.00 – 275.00

The "Envoy" was selected to be in the King's Flight (King George VI) in 1938 and was fitted out as the King's personal transport. Dinky made this model special and painted it in colors of the Brigade of the Guards.

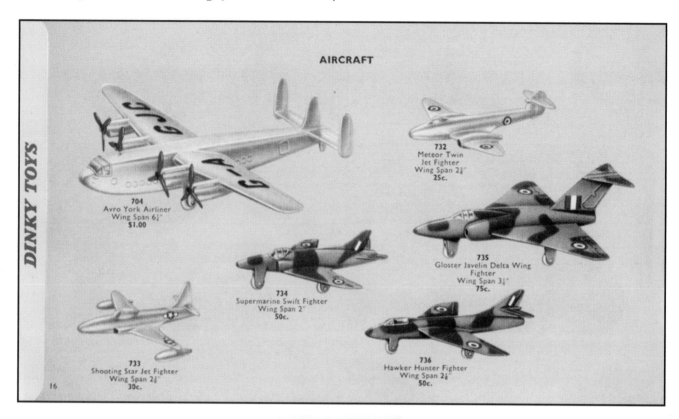

Dinky toy catalog.

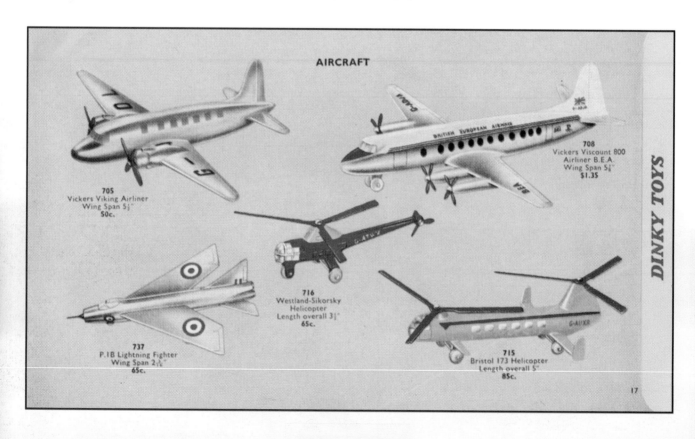

Dinky toy catalog.

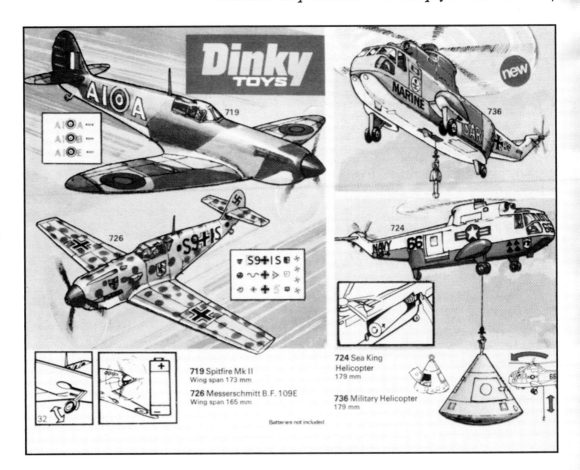

Dinky toy catalog, 1973.

719 Spitfire Mk II
Wing span 173 mm

726 Messerschmitt B.F. 109E
Wing span 165 mm

Batteries not included

724 Sea King
Helicopter
179 mm

736 Military Helicopter
179 mm

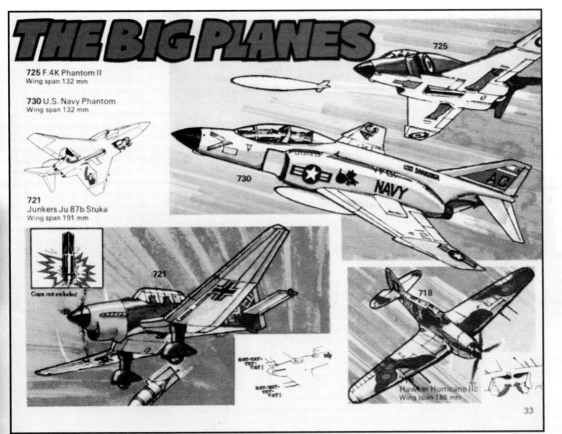

THE BIG PLANES

725 F.4K Phantom II
Wing span 132 mm

730 U.S. Navy Phantom
Wing span 132 mm

721
Junkers Ju 87b Stuka
Wing span 191 mm

Caps not included

Hawker Hurricane IIc
Wing span 188 mm

Dinky toy catalog, 1973.

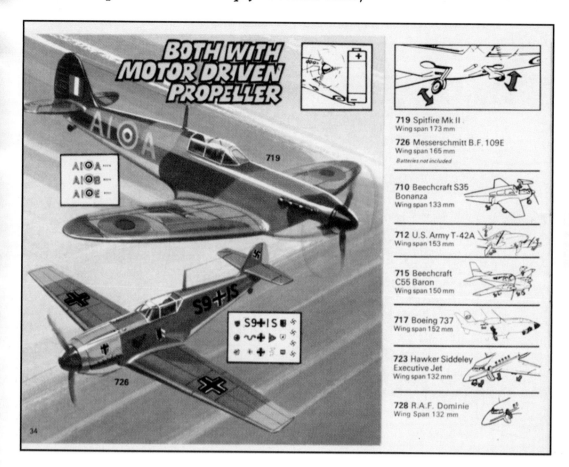

719 Spitfire Mk II
Wing span 173 mm

726 Messerschmitt B.F. 109E
Wing span 165 mm
Batteries not included

710 Beechcraft S35
Bonanza
Wing span 133 mm

712 U.S. Army T-42A
Wing span 153 mm

715 Beechcraft
C55 Baron
Wing span 150 mm

717 Boeing 737
Wing span 152 mm

723 Hawker Siddeley
Executive Jet
Wing span 132 mm

728 R.A.F. Dominie
Wing Span 132 mm

*Dinky toy catalog,
1974.*

*Dinky toy catalog,
1974.*

Dinky toy catalog.

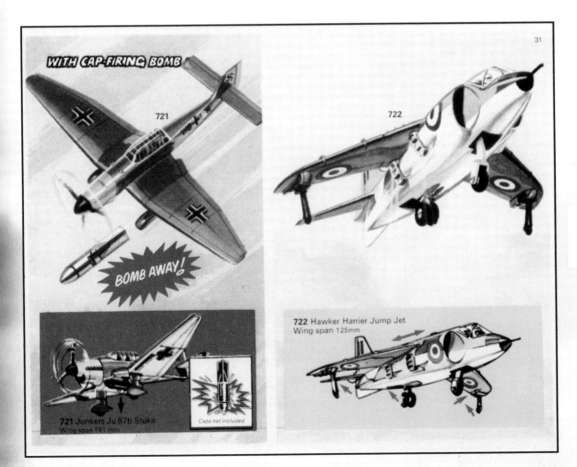

Dinky toy catalog.

Dinky toy catalog, 1976.

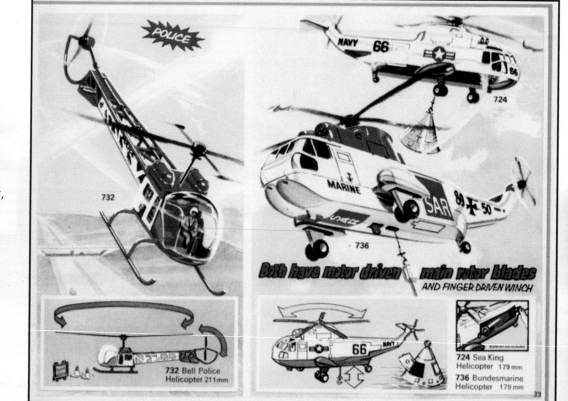

Dinky toy catalog, 1976.

Edison Giocattoli, S.p.A., Italy

Model:	Fokker triplane DR.I
Year:	1970s
Wingspan:	4"
Price Range:	$75.00 – 100.00

This miniature DR.I is an attractive and detailed model of the plane used by the famous "Red Baron" of Germany in World War I.

Model:	S.P.A.D. XIII Scout
Year:	1970s
Wingspan	4½"
Price Range:	$50.00 – 75.00

Model:	Ansaldo SVA Scout
Year:	1970s
Wingspan	4¼"
Price Range:	$35.00 – 75.00

Model:	Nieuport 17
Year:	1970s
Wingspan:	4"
Price Range:	$35.00 – 75.00

Model:	Royal Air Force SE5A
Year:	1970s
Wingspan:	4½"
Price Range:	$35.00 – 75.00

Model:	Aviatik D. I
Year:	1970s
Wingspan:	4¼"
Price Range:	$35.00 – 75.00

Model:	Sopwith "Baby" floatplane
Year:	1970s
Wingspan:	4¼"
Price Range:	$35.00 – 75.00

Model:	Hansa "Brandenberg" D.I.
Year:	1970s
Wingspan:	4½"
Price Range:	$35.00 – 75.00

Model:	Macchi Castoldi M.C. 72
Year:	1970s
Wingspan:	4½"
Price Range:	$100.00 – 150.00

Seaplane speedster from Italy in 1933 set a world's speed record of 423 mph. Counter-rotating propellers offset torque with the powerful 2,500 hp. engines used in this Macchi 72.

Model:	Supermarine S-5
Year:	1970s
Wingspan:	4½"
Price Range:	$100.00 – 150.00

Model:	Gee Bee "Z"
Year:	1970s
Wingspan:	4¼"
Price Range:	$100.00 – 150.00

Pilot Lowell Bayles flew the "Z" to win the Thompson Trophy Race in 1931.

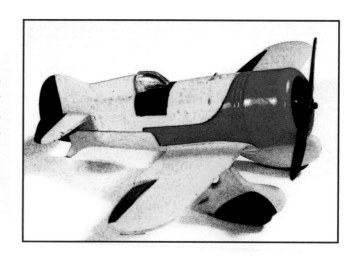

Erie (Parker White Metal), Erie, Pennsylvania

A manufacturer of slush-cast toys that all appeared on the market prior to W.W.II. These toys were a popular item in the nickel and dime stores (Woolworth, Kresge, Franklin, etc.).

Model:	Boeing B-17
Year:	1930s
Wingspan:	6¼"
Price Range:	$80.00 – 120.00

Model:	Boeing 247
Year:	1930s
Wingspan:	3½"
Price Range:	$100.00 – 125.00

Model:	Northrop "Delta"
Year:	1930s
Wingspan:	6"
Price Range:	$150.00 – 250.00

Model:	Northrop "Gamma"
Year:	1930s
Wingspan:	6"
Price Range:	$150.00 – 250.00

Model:	Northrop "Beta" monoplane
Year:	1930s
Wingspan:	4"
Price Range:	$100.00 – 150.00

The ERTL Co., Dyersville, Iowa

Model:	Douglas DC-3
Year:	1990
Wingspan:	16"
Price Range:	$100.00 – 150.00

ERTL's DC-3 model is a large and detailed replica of the real airplane. Among the toy planes that have been built, this model stands out from the pack because of the care given to its detailed design.

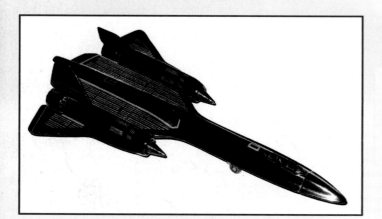

Model:	Lockheed "Blackbird" SR-71
Year:	1987
Wingspan:	5"
Price Range:	$25.00 – 40.00

Model:	Rockwell B-1 Bomber
Year:	1987
Wingspan:	9"
Price Range:	$25.00 – 40.00

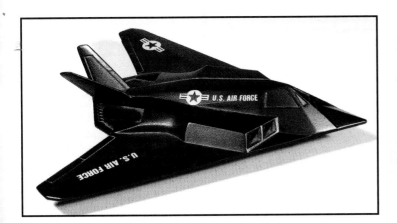

Model:	Lockheed "Nighthawk" F-117
Year:	1998
Wingspan:	6"
Price Range:	$20.00 – 35.00

This model of the F-117 is a close likeness to the real "Nighthawk" and it shows the angular shape used to deflect radar rays for stealth in flight.

Model:	Early Stealth Design
Year:	1988
Wingspan:	3¼"
Price Range:	$25.00 – 35.00

Model:	Hawker "Harrier"
Year:	N.A.
Wingspan:	2¾"
Price Range:	$15.00 – 25.00

Model:	MIG-29
Year:	1990
Wingspan:	5½"
Price Range:	$15.00 – 25.00

Model:	Fairchild-Republic "Thunderbolt II"
Year:	1988
Wingspan:	6¾"
Price Range:	$15.00 – 25.00

Model:	McDonnell F-4 "Phantom"
Year:	1988
Wingspan:	5"
Price Range:	$15.00 – 25.00

Model:	McDonnell F-15 "Eagle"
Year:	1991
Wingspan:	4½"
Price Range:	$15.00 – 25.00

Model:	General Dynamics F-16 "Falcon"
Year:	1987
Wingspan:	4¾"
Price Range:	$15.00 – 25.00

Model:	McDonnell-Douglas F-18 "Hornet"
Year:	1989
Wingspan:	5 "
Price Range:	$15.00 – 25.00

Model:	Grumman F-14 "Tomcat"
Year	1987
Wingspan:	7¼"
Price Range:	$15.00 – 25.00

Model:	Boeing 707 USAF #1
Year:	1989
Wingspan:	5"
Price Range:	$10.00 – 20.00

Model:	Douglas DC-9
Year:	N.A.
Wingspan:	4"
Price Range:	$10.00 – 20.00

Model:	Douglas DC-10
Year:	N.A.
Wingspan:	5½"
Price Range:	$10.00 – 20.00

Model:	Boeing 737
Year:	N.A.
Wingspan:	4½"
Price Range:	$10.00 – 20.00

Model:	McDonnell F-15 "Eagle"
Year:	1988
Wingspan:	13"
Price Range:	$20.00 – 35.00

A large model of the F-15, made of both metal and plastic. Later versions were entirely plastic.

Model:	Eurofighter
Year:	N.A.
Wingspan:	4½"
Price Range:	$10.00 – 30.00

Franklin Mint, Franklin Center, Pennsylvania

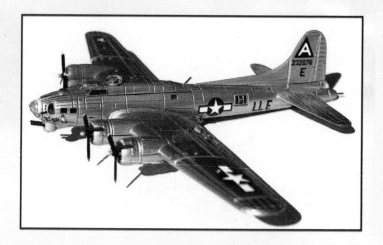

Model:	Boeing B-17
Year:	1990
Wingspan:	13"
Price Range:	$150.00 – 200.00

This large, detailed model of the B-17 shows features of the real aircraft which never show up on other models. Details such as landing gear and armament can be observed on the model. A fine exhibit of W.W.II airpower.

Formerly built in China, the Armour collection has been acquired by Franklin Mint in the United States. Made of a heavy metal, these diecast models are quite detailed and have elaborate and authentic paint designs that depict color schemes of certain World War II aces.

Model:	Focke-Wulf Fw 190
Year:	2000
Wingspan:	8"
Price Range:	$50.00 – 100.00

Model:	Junkers "Stuka" Ju 87
Year:	2000
Wingspan:	11½"
Price Range:	$50.00 – 100.00

Model:	Messerschmitt Bf 109
Year:	2001
Wingspan:	8"
Price Range:	$50.00 – 100.00

The paint design on this Bf 109 was used by Germany's top World War II ace Lieutenant Erich Hartman, who scored 352 victories against Russian forces at the Eastern front.

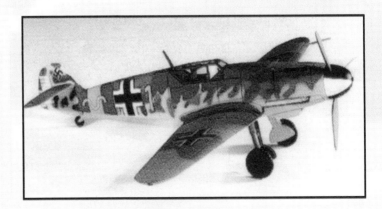

Gabriel Mfg. Co., Lancaster, Pennsylvania

Model:	Beech "Twin Bonanza"
Year:	1970s
Wingspan:	10¾"
Price Range:	$30.00 – 50.00

This design is a likeness of the "Twin Bonanza" except for the tail which was borrowed from the "Bonanza." This toy has an airstair that opens. The Gabriel Co. was the successor to Hubley in Lancaster, Pennsylvania.

Goodee Mfg. Co., U.S.A.

Model:	Douglas C-54
Year:	N.A.
Wingspan:	5½"
Price Range:	$5.00 – 10.00

Model:	F-94 jet fighter
Year:	1970s
Wingspan:	4"
Price Range:	$5.00 – 10.00

Hubley Mfg., Lancaster, Pennsylvania

Following the decline of cast iron toy production, Hubley transitioned to diecast toys, and remained prominent among the toy manufacturers with the airplane toys that were related to the planes of W.W. II.

Model:	Lockheed P-38 "Lightning"
Year:	1962
Wingspan:	13"
Price Range:	$150.00 – 200.00

A favorite of young boys this detailed model has retractible wheels and is a realistic copy of the real aircraft.

Model:	Navy Fighter/Bomber "Hellcat"
Year:	1956
Wingspan:	11"
Price Range:	$80.00 – 125.00

Later production models were termed "American Eagle" and were made by Scale Models Co. from Hubley dies. The model's wings fold up and the plane has retractible landing gear.

Model:	Army Fighter
Year:	1940
Wingspan:	5½"
Price Range:	$50.00 – 75.00

Model:	Brewster "Buffalo"
Year:	1953
Wingspan:	8½"
Price Range:	$50.00 – 75.00

Model:	Bell P-39 "Airacobra"
Year:	1941
Wingspan:	5½"
Price Range:	$50.00 – 75.00

Model:	Bell "Airacuda"
Year:	1940
Wingspan:	10"
Price Range:	$250.00 – 350.00

The "Airacuda" is a rare item in Hubley's line. An airplane that was built for the U.S. military in the 1930s, the design did not receive production orders, but it was a novel concept with gun turrets over the wing.

Model:	Piper "Cub"
Year:	1963
Wingspan:	8"
Price Range:	$50.00 – 75.00

Model:	Curtiss P-40 "Warhawk"
Year:	1962
Wingspan:	8¼"
Price Range:	$80.00 – 150.00

Model:	Douglas F-6 "Skyray"
Year:	1969
Wingspan:	6"
Price Range:	$50.00 – 75.00

Model:	Seversky P-35
Year:	1939
Wingspan:	8"
Price Range:	$50.00 – 75.00

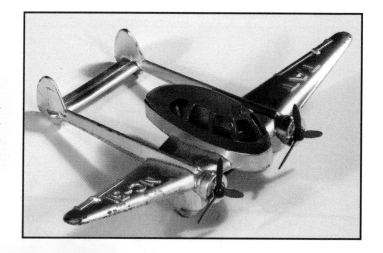

Model:	"Crusader"
Year:	1936
Wingspan:	5"
Price Range:	$50.00 – 85.00

Model:	Lockheed P-80
Year:	1955
Wingspan:	6"
Price Range:	$45.00 – 75.00

Model:	Lockheed "Electra"
Year:	N.A.
Wingspan:	4¼"
Price Range:	$45.00 – 75.00

Kansas Toy & Novelty Co., Clifton, Kansas

Kansas Toy was started by Art Haynes in 1923. He made his own designs and molds and produced many slush-cast white metal toys which were ultimately sold through the dime stores of that time. Kansas Toy produced toy autos and planes until 1935.

Model:	Cabin monoplane
Year:	N.A.
Wingspan:	2¼"
Price Range:	$20.00 – 30.00

Model:	Monoplane
Year:	N.A.
Wingspan:	2¼"
Price Range:	$20.00 – 30.00

Model:	Fokker T-2
Year:	N.A.
Wingspan:	3"
Price Range:	$30.00 – 50.00

Model:	Cabin Transport
Year:	N.A.
Wingspan:	2¾"
Price Range:	$35.00 – 65.00

Model:	Primary Glider
Year:	1930s
Wingspan:	2½"
Price Range:	$50.00 – 75.00

KEJ Mfg. Co., N.A.

Model:	Transport plane
Year:	N.A.
Wingspan:	6½"
Price Range:	$50.00 – 80.00

This transport was cast from a heavy metal, probably lead.

Lincoln White Metal Works, Lincoln, Nebraska

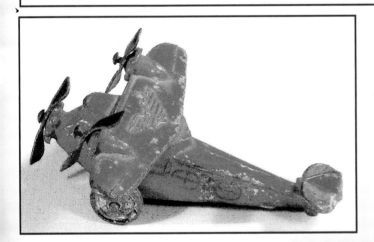

Starting in 1931, Clayton Stevenson produced many slush-cast toys that were marketed through the nation's dime stores until 1940.

Model:	Trimotor
Year:	1930s
Wingspan:	2½"
Price Range:	$50.00 – 80.00

Lintoy-South Asia Industries, Hong Kong

Model:	Saab "Draken"
Year:	1970s
Wingspan:	4"
Price Range:	$20.00 – 30.00

Model:	Grumman F11F "Tiger"
Year:	1970s
Wingspan:	4"
Price Range:	$20.00 – 35.00

Model:	Douglas DC-10
Year:	1970s
Wingspan:	4½ "
Price Range:	$20.00 – 35.00

Model:	Lockheed 1011
Year:	1970s
Wingspan:	5"
Price Range:	$20.00 – 35.00

Model:	North Amer. P-51
Year:	1970s
Wingspan:	5¼"
Price Range:	$20.00 – 35.00

Model:	Douglas A-20
Year:	1970s
Wingspan:	5¼"
Price Range:	$20.00 – 35.00

Model:	Messerschmidt ME-262
Year:	1970s
Wingspan:	5"
Price Range:	$20.00 – 35.00

An unusual plane, this late W.W.II German jet is presently being built in a full-scale flying aircraft for business flying, and airshow use at an airfield near Seattle, Washington.

Model:	Mitsubishi "Zero"
Year:	1970s
Wingspan:	5"
Price Range:	$20.00 – 35.00

Model:	Piper "Navajo"
Year:	1970s
Wingspan:	6"
Price Range:	$20.00 – 35.00

Model:	Boeing 747 w/ Shuttle
Year:	1970s
Wingspan:	5"
Price Range:	$20.00 – 35.00

This setup is used to carry the Space Shuttle back to its Florida home base if conditions prevent landing at the Florida site. The cranes and jigs used to place the shuttle atop the 747 are impressively enormous.

Model:	Lear jet
Year:	1970s
Wingspan:	4"
Price Range:	$20.00 – 35.00

Model:	Piper "Cherokee"
Year:	1970s
Wingspan:	5"
Price Range:	$20.00 – 35.00

Model:	deHavilland "Comet I"
Year:	1970s
Wingspan:	5"
Price Range:	$20.00 – 35.00

Model:	North Amer. B-25
Year:	1970s
Wingspan:	5"
Price Range:	$20.00 – 35.00

Model:	Republic P-47
Year:	1970s
Wingspan:	5"
Price Range:	$20.00 – 35.00

Model:	Boeing 747
Year:	1970s
Wingspan:	5"
Price Range:	$20.00 – 35.00

London Toy Museum, Britain

Model:	Avro "Vulcan"
Year:	N.A.
Wingspan:	3¼"
Price Range:	$100.00 – 150.00

Londontoy Ltd., Britain

Model:	Hawker "Hurricane"
Year:	N.A.
Wingspan:	4½"
Price Range:	$40.00 – 90.00

Maisto Intl. Inc., Fontana, California

Model:	Convair B-24
Year:	1997
Wingspan:	6"
Price Range:	$5.00 – 15.00

Mak A Plane, Britain

Model:	Boulton "Defiant"
Year:	N.A.
Wingspan:	4¾"
Price Range:	$40.00 – 80.00

Matchbox-Lesney Products, Britain

Beginning in 1948, Matchbox toys have been produced and marketed in the world market. They produce autos, work vehicles, and toy planes.

Model:	LTV "Corsair," A-7
Year:	1980s
Wingspan:	3¼"
Price Range:	$10.00 – 20.00

Model:	Douglas "Skyhawk" A-4
Year:	1980s
Wingspan:	3"
Price Range:	$10.00 – 20.00

Model:	Hawker "Harrier"
Year:	1980s
Wingspan:	2¾"
Price Range:	$10.00 – 20.00

Model:	Dassault "Mirage"
Year:	1980s
Wingspan:	2½"
Price Range:	$10.00 – 20.00

Model:	Cessna 402
Year:	1980s
Wingspan:	4"
Price Range:	$10.00 – 20.00

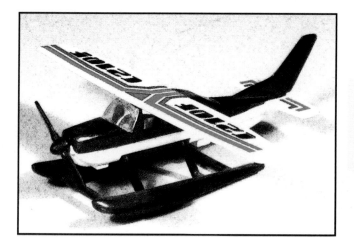

Model:	Cessna 210 floatplane
Year:	1980s
Wingspan:	4"
Price Range:	$10.00 – 20.00

Model:	Grumman "Tomcat" F-14
Year:	1980s
Wingspan:	3"
Price Range:	$10.00 – 20.00

Model:	"Concorde" SST
Year:	1980s
Wingspan:	2"
Price Range:	$10.00 – 20.00

Model:	"Wild Wind" racer
Year:	1980s
Wingspan:	4"
Price Range:	$10.00 – 20.00

Model:	Hawker "Bucaneer"
Year:	1980s
Wingspan:	3"
Price Range:	$10.00 – 20.00

Model:	Lear jet
Year:	1980s
Wingspan:	3¼"
Price Range:	$10.00 – 20.00

Model:	Pitts "Special"
Year:	1980s
Wingspan:	4"
Price Range:	$10.00 – 20.00

Model:	Airbus 300
Year:	1980s
Wingspan:	3"
Price Range:	$10.00 – 20.00

Model:	Douglas DC-10
Year:	1980s
Wingspan:	3"
Price Range:	$10.00 – 20.00

Model:	Alpha jet
Year:	1980s
Wingspan:	3"
Price Range:	$10.00 – 20.00

Model:	Lockheed F-104
Year:	1980s
Wingspan:	2¼"
Price Range:	$10.00 – 20.00

Model:	General Dynamics F-16
Year:	1980s
Wingspan:	3"
Price Range:	$10.00 – 20.00

Model:	Cessna 210
Year:	1980s
Wingspan:	3"
Price Range:	$10.00 – 20.00

Matchbox catalog, 1979 – 1980.

Model:	English Electric "Lightning"
Year:	1980s
Wingspan:	3"
Price Range:	$10.00 – 20.00

Matchbox catalog, 1986.

Mattel, U.S.A.

Model:	"Cloud Hopper"
Year:	1970s
Wingspan:	3½"
Price Range:	$7.00 – 15.00

Model:	"Mach Bird"
Year:	1970s
Wingspan:	4"
Price Range:	$7.00 – 15.00

Model:	"Metal Eagle"
Year:	1970s
Wingspan:	3½"
Price Range:	$7.00 – 15.00

Mercury, Italy

Model:	Convair B-36
Year:	1970s
Wingspan:	10"
Price Range:	$200.00 – 250.00

This B-36 is a unique toy plane model as it is the only solid casting model of this unusually large airplane. Later versions of the B-36 had jet engines attached to the wing.

Model:	Convair F-7U "Cutlass"
Year:	1970s
Wingspan:	2½"
Price Range:	$50.00 – 75.00

Model:	North Amer. F-86 "Sabrejet"
Year:	1970s
Wingspan:	2"
Price Range:	$50.00 – 75.00

Model:	Fiat G-80
Year:	1970s
Wingspan:	2"
Price Range:	$50.00 – 75.00

Midgetoy, U.S.A.

Midgetoy planes have open bodies without a bottom to the fuselage. This type of casting simplifies the molding process and saves on material.

Model:	Boeing 707
Year:	1970s
Wingspan:	4½"
Price Range:	$15.00 – 30.00

Model:	Grumman F-9 "Cougar"
Year:	1970s
Wingspan:	3¼"
Price Range:	$10.00 – 20.00

Model:	North Amer. F-86 "Sabrejet"
Year:	1970s
Wingspan:	4"
Price Range:	$10.00 – 20.00

Model:	Martin "Canberra"
Year:	1970s
Wingspan:	3½"
Price Range:	$15.00 – 30.00

Nakajima (NKJ), Japan

Model:	McDonnell F-4 "Phantom"
Year:	1980s
Wingspan:	5"
Price Range:	$100.00 – 150.00

Model:	McDonnell-Douglas F-15 "Eagle"
Year:	1980s
Wingspan:	5½"
Price Range:	$120.00 – 150.00

NZG Modelle, Germany

Model:	Lockheed "Orion"
Year:	1983
Wingspan:	5¼"
Price Range:	$100.00 – 150.00

This delightful model of the "Orion" was built for a special anniversary of SAS Airlines. A realistic likeness of the "Orion," the model in miniature was made in limited quantity and sold only to SAS. Somehow some exceptions escaped and made their way into a few collections.

Precision Acco Casting, U.S.A.

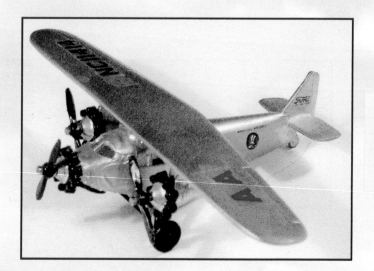

Model:	Ford trimotor
Year:	N.A.
Wingspan:	4½"
Price Range:	$90.00 – 150.00

Model:	Douglas DC-3
Year:	N.A.
Wingspan:	5"
Price Range:	$90.00 – 150.00

Renwal Mfg. Co., U.S.A. (1939 – 1970)

Model:	Lockheed "Constellation"
Year:	N.A.
Wingspan:	8"
Price Range:	$100.00 – 150.00

Model:	Republic F-94 "Thunderjet"
Year:	N.A.
Wingspan:	7"
Price Range:	$50.00 – 75.00

Revell Inc., Des Plaines, Illinois

Model:	MIG-29
Year:	1990
Wingspan:	4½"
Price Range:	$25.00 – 45.00

Model:	Eurofighter
Year:	1990
Wingspan:	4¾"
Price Range:	$25.00 – 45.00

Model:	"Flanker" SU-27
Year:	1990
Wingspan:	4¾"
Price Range:	$25.00 – 45.00

Model:	McDonnell-Douglas F-15 "Eagle"
Year:	1991
Wingspan:	4½"
Price Range:	$25.00 – 45.00

Model:	McDonnell-Douglas F-18 "Hornet"
Year:	1991
Wingspan:	5"
Price Range:	$25.00 – 45.00

Model:	General Dynamics F-16 "Falcon"
Year:	1991
Wingspan:	4½"
Price Range:	$25.00 – 45.00

Schabak Mfg. Co., Germany

The Schabak line has miniatures of many airline transports. Although small in size, the castings are realistic and the toys are very nicely finished with a good paint job and good registration of screened detail of airline markings. On the very small planes, the detail shown is quite remarkable for the mass production runs made and the size of the planes (note wingspans).

Model:	Douglas DC-3
Year:	1980s
Wingspan:	4½"
Price Range:	$10.00 – 20.00

Model:	Douglas DC-3
Year:	1980s
Wingspan:	1½"
Price Range:	$10.00 – 20.00

Model:	Junkers Ju-52
Year:	1980s
Wingspan:	4½"
Price Range:	$15.00 – 30.00

Model:	Convair CV-440
Year:	1980s
Wingspan:	2"
Price Range:	$10.00 – 20.00

Model:	Fairchild F-27
Year:	1980s
Wingspan:	2"
Price Range:	$10.00 – 20.00

Model:	ATR-42
Year:	1980s
Wingspan:	2"
Price Range:	$10.00 – 20.00

Model:	Lockheed "Constellation"
Year:	1980s
Wingspan:	2¼"
Price Range:	$15.00 – 30.00

Model:	Fokker F-28
Year:	1990s
Wingspan :	2"
Price Range:	$10.00 – 20.00

Model:	Embraer 120
Year:	1990s
Wingspan:	1¼"
Price Range:	$10.00 – 20.00

Model:	Boeing 727
Year:	1980s
Wingspan:	2¼"
Price Range:	$15.00 – 30.00

Model:	Boeing 737
Year:	1980s
Wingspan:	2"
Price Range:	$10.00 – 20.00

Model:	Boeing 747
Year:	1980s
Wingspan:	4"
Price Range:	$15.00 – 30.00

Model:	Boeing 757
Year:	1980s
Wingspan:	2½"
Price Range:	$15.00 – 30.00

Model:	Boeing 767
Year:	1980s
Wingspan:	3½"
Price Range:	$15.00 – 30.00

Model:	Boeing 777
Year:	1990s
Wingspan:	4"
Price Range:	$15.00 – 30.00

Model:	Douglas DC-9
Year:	1980s
Wingspan:	2¼"
Price Range:	$15.00 – 30.00

Model:	Douglas DC-10
Year:	1980s
Wingspan:	3"
Price Range:	$15.00 – 30.00

Model:	Lockheed 1011
Year:	1980s
Wingspan:	3"
Price Range:	$15.00 – 30.00

Model:	Airbus 300
Year:	1980s
Wingspan:	3"
Price Range:	$15.00 – 30.00

Model:	Boeing 707, USAF #1
Year:	1980s
Wingspan:	3"
Price Range:	$15.00 – 30.00

Model:	Airbus A310
Year:	1980s
Wingspan:	3"
Price Range:	$15.00 – 30.00

Model:	Airbus A340
Year:	1990s
Wingspan:	4"
Price Range:	$15.00 – 25.00

Schuco Mfg. Co., Germany

Model:	Ilushin IL-62
Year:	1970s
Wingspan:	3"
Price Range:	$35.00 – 50.00

Model:	Junkers JU-52
Year:	1980s
Wingspan:	3"
Price Range:	$20.00 – 30.00

Model:	Potez "Magister" 170
Year:	1970s
Wingspan:	5¾"
Price Range:	$100.00 – 125.00

Model:	Republic F-84
Year:	1970s
Wingspan:	5"
Price Range:	$100.00 – 125.00

Model:	Douglas F-6 "Skyray"
Year:	1970s
Wingspan:	4"
Price Range:	$100.00 – 125.00

Model:	Douglas F-6 "Skyray"
Year:	1970s
Wingspan:	1¾"
Price Range:	$35.00 – 50.00

Model:	Republic F-84
Year:	1970s
Wingspan:	2"
Price Range:	$35.00 – 50.00

Solido Mfg. Co., France

Model:	Sud "Vatour" II
Year:	N.A.
Wingspan:	4"
Price Range:	$35.00 – 50.00

Model:	Douglas F-6 "Skyray"
Year:	N.A.
Wingspan:	2½"
Price Range:	$35.00 – 50.00

T & B, Britain

Model:	T&B monoplane
Year:	1930s
Wingspan:	4"
Price Range:	$100.00 – 150.00

Tekno, Dansk Legetojs Industri, Denmark (1928)

Model:	Light-twin ambulance
Year:	1938
Wingspan:	8"
Price Range:	$200.00 – 300.00

Model:	Douglas DC-7C
Year:	1970s
Wingspan:	7¾"
Price Range:	$250.00 – 300.00

The DC-7C is a precise made toy with great appeal because of its detail, and it is one of a few airliners of the age before jets that had an influence on the increase in air transportation.

Model:	Douglas SBD
Year:	1940s
Wingspan:	3½"
Price Range:	$50.00 – 100.00

Model:	North Amer. F-100 "Super Sabre"
Year:	1970s
Wingspan:	3½"
Price Range:	$150.00 – 200.00

Another super model which appeals to the collector due to its attention to detail and a model which holds special interest to a collector that is fascinated with military models.

Model:	MIG-15
Year:	1970s
Wingspan:	3¼"
Price Range:	$85.00 – 125.00

Model:	Dassault "Mystere"
Year:	1970s
Wingspan:	3¼"
Price Range:	$75.00 – 125.00

Model:	Boeing B-17
Year:	N.A.
Wingspan:	5¾"
Price Range:	$100.00 – 200.00

Model:	Hawker "Hunter"
Year:	1970s
Wingspan:	3¼"
Price Range:	$90.00 – 150.00

Timpo Toys, Great Britain

Model:	Boeing B-17
Year:	N.A.
Wingspan:	5"
Price Range:	$25.00 – 50.00

Model:	Lockheed P-38
Year:	N.A.
Wingspan:	4"
Price Range:	$20.00 – 40.00

Tin Toys, Hong Kong

Model:	MIG-15
Year:	N.A.
Wingspan:	4"
Price Range:	$10.00 – 20.00

Tonka Toys (1947 – 1963)

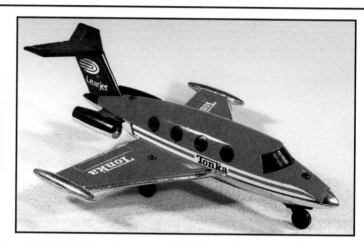

Model:	Lear jet
Year:	N.A.
Wingspan:	7"
Price Range:	$25.00 – 50.00

Tootsietoy (Strombecker Corp.), Chicago, Illinois

Tootsietoy began in 1876 as a publishing firm, and printed the National Laundry Journal. Later they began making accessories including collar buttons. A newly designed type casting machine in 1893 had possibilities for casting the collar button from type lead. Success at this venture put the company at the head of the die cast industry. Next, simple diecast toys were made and the progression into all sorts of autos, trains, trucks, and planes for the youth market put Tootsietoy at the top of toy manufacturers in the United States. They continue even today to provide low cost toys.

Model:	Bleriot monoplane
Year:	1910
Wingspan:	2½"
Price Range:	$50.00 – 75.00

Model:	JN-4 biplane
Year:	1926
Wingspan:	2¼"
Price Range:	$100.00 – 150.00

Model:	Aero Dawn monoplane
Year:	1934
Wingspan:	3¾"
Price Range:	$50.00 – 75.00

Model:	Aero Dawn biplane
Year:	1932
Wingspan:	4"
Price Range:	$50.00 – 75.00

Model:	U.S. Navy Waco
Year:	1937
Wingspan:	5"
Price Range:	$75.00 – 100.00

Model:	Dive bomber Waco
Year:	1937
Wingspan:	5"
Price Range:	$200.00 – 250.00

Model:	Lockheed "Sirius"
Year:	1932
Wingspan:	3½"
Price Range:	$50.00 – 85.00

Model:	Lockheed "Electra"
Year:	1937
Wingspan:	4"
Price Range:	$50.00 – 75.00

Model:	Aero Dawn floatplane
Year:	1932
Wingspan:	3¾"
Price Range:	$75.00 – 100.00

Model:	Ford trimotor
Year:	1932
Wingspan:	5¼"
Price Range:	$125.00 – 150.00

Model:	Douglas DC-2
Year:	1936
Wingspan:	5¼"
Price Range:	$75.00 – 125.00

Model:	Pitcarin Autogiro
Year:	1934
Wingspan:	4½"
Price Range:	$100.00 – 150.00

Model:	Zepplin "U.S. Los Angeles"
Year:	1937
Wingspan:	5"
Price Range:	$125.00 – 150.00

Model:	Army pursuit
Year:	1936
Wingspan:	4"
Price Range:	$35.00 – 65.00

Model:	"Crusader"
Year:	1937
Wingspan:	5¼"
Price Range:	$75.00 – 100.00

Model:	Piper "Cub"
Year:	1948
Wingspan:	4"
Price Range:	$35.00 – 65.00

Model:	North Amer. "Navion"
Year:	1948
Wingspan:	4¼"
Price Range:	$35.00 – 65.00

Model:	Douglas DC-4 U.S. Army
Year:	1941
Wingspan:	5¼"
Price Range:	$75.00 – 125.00

Model:	Convair liner 240
Year:	1950
Wingspan:	5¼"
Price Range:	$75.00 – 100.00

Model:	Lockheed P-38
Year:	1950
Wingspan:	5"
Price Range:	$100.00 – 125.00

Model:	Boeing "Stratocruiser" 377
Year:	1951
Wingspan:	6½"
Price Range:	$100.00 – 150.00

Model:	Lockheed "Constellation"
Year:	1951
Wingspan:	5½"
Price Range:	$100.00 – 150.00

Model:	Beechcraft "Bonanza"
Year:	1948
Wingspan:	4"
Price Range:	$30.00 – 50.00

Model:	Lockheed P-80
Year:	1948
Wingspan:	4¼"
Price Range:	$30.00 – 50.00

Model:	Grummon "Tomcat" F-14
Year:	N.A.
Wingspan:	1½"
Price Range:	$1.00 – 5.00

Model:	Northrop F-5 "Tiger"
Year:	1970
Wingspan:	2½"
Price Range:	$10.00 – 20.00

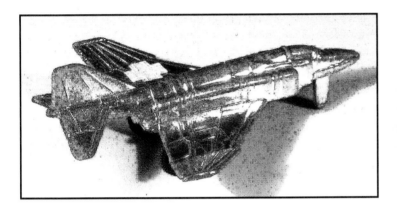

Model:	McDonnell F-4 "Phantom"
Year:	1970
Wingspan:	2½"
Price Range:	$10.00 – 20.00

Model:	Boeing 707
Year:	1958
Wingspan:	6"
Price Range:	$30.00 – 50.00

Model:	Grumman F9F "Panther"
Year:	1956
Wingspan:	3½"
Price Range:	$10.00 – 20.00

Model:	Vought F7U "Cutlass"
Year:	1956
Wingspan:	3¾"
Price Range:	$10.00 – 20.00

Model:	Lockheed F-94 "Starfire"
Year:	1956
Wingspan:	3½"
Price Range:	$10.00 – 20.00

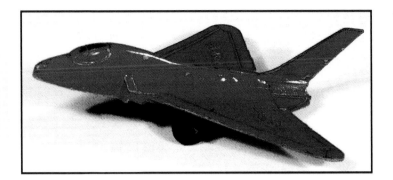

Model:	Douglas F-6 "Skyray"
Year:	1956
Wingspan:	3"
Price Range:	$10.00 – 20.00

Model:	Vought F4U "Corsair"
Year:	1979
Wingspan:	6½"
Price Range:	$15.00 – 25.00

Model:	Sailplane
Year:	N.A.
Wingspan:	6½"
Price Range:	$25.00 – 50.00

Model:	Boeing B-17
Year:	1988
Wingspan:	4"
Price Range:	$10.00 – 15.00

Model:	Fokker DR-1 triplane
Year:	N.A.
Wingspan:	9"
Price Range:	$50.00 – 75.00

Model:	Curtiss P-40 "Warhawk"
Year:	N.A.
Wingspan:	6½"
Price Range:	$10.00 – 20.00

Model:	Martin B-26 "Marauder"
Year:	N.A.
Wingspan:	10½"
Price Range:	$25.00 – 40.00

Model:	Bell P-39 "Airacobra"
Year:	1947
Wingspan:	5¼"
Price Range:	$75.00 – 125.00

Model:	Delta jet
Year:	1954
Wingspan:	2¾"
Price Range:	$30.00 – 45.00

Model:	Bleriot monoplane
Year:	1936
Wingspan:	¾"
Price Range:	$35.00 – 50.00

Model:	Douglas DC-4 "Mainliner"
Year:	1941
Wingspan:	5¼"
Price Range:	$75.00 – 100.00

Model:	Monoplane
Year:	1936
Wingspan:	1½"
Price Range:	$10.00 – 20.00

Model:	General Dynamics F-16
Year:	1980s
Wingspan:	5"
Price Range:	$10.00 – 20.00

Union Model Co., Japan

Model:	Gee Bee "Super R" racer
Year:	1988
Wingspan:	6"
Price Range:	$30.00 – 50.00

Universal Mfg. Co.

Model:	Vought "Corsair" F4U
Year:	N.A.
Wingspan:	4¼"
Price Range:	$15.00 – 25.00

Model:	Curtiss P-40 "Warhawk"
Year:	N.A.
Wingspan:	4"
Price Range:	$15.00 – 25.00

Model:	Supermarine "Spitfire"
Year:	N.A.
Wingspan:	4¼"
Price Range:	$15.00 – 25.00

C. A. Woods Novelty Co., Clay Center, Kansas (1925 – 1940)

Model:	Fokker T-2
Year:	N.A.
Wingspan:	3¼"
Price Range:	$40.00 – 65.00

Model:	Northrop "Alpha"
Year:	1930s
Wingspan:	2¾"
Price Range:	$50.00 – 75.00

Model:	Northrop "Alpha"
Year:	1930s
Wingspan:	4"
Price Range:	$60.00 – 85.00

Model:	Northrop "Altair"
Year:	1930s
Wingspan:	4"
Price Range:	$60.00 – 85.00

Model:	"Mr. Mulligan"
Year:	1930s
Wingspan:	3¼"
Price Range:	$75.00 – 125.00

A tribute to Benny Howard's famous racer "Mr. Mulligan" which won the Thompson Trophy and Bendix Trophy races in 1935, this toy was a popular item in that era.

Model:	Douglas "Dolphin" amphibian
Year:	1930s
Wingspan:	4"
Price Range:	$50.00 – 85.00

Model:	Douglas "Dolphin" amphibian
Year:	1930s
Wingspan:	2½"
Price Range:	$50.00 – 75.00

Model:	Ford trimotor
Year:	1930s
Wingspan:	5¼"
Price Range:	$100.00 – 150.00

Model:	Boeing 247
Year:	1930s
Wingspan:	3½"
Price Range:	$35.00 – 60.00

This toy resembles the Boeing 247, and has "Boeing and NC13361" on the top of the wing.

Zee/Zylnex, Hong Kong

Model:	Republic F-84
Year:	N.A.
Wingspan:	2¾"
Price Range:	$10.00 – 20.00

Model:	Futs biplane
Year:	N.A.
Wingspan:	3½"
Price Range:	$10.00 – 20.00

Model:	Grumman "Albatross"
Year:	N.A.
Wingspan:	3¾"
Price Range:	$10.00 – 20.00

Model:	Rockwell OV-10 "Bronco"
Year:	N.A.
Wingspan:	3¾"
Price Range:	$10.00 – 20.00

Model:	Grumman E-2 "Hawkeye"
Year:	N.A.
Wingspan:	2½"
Price Range:	$10.00 – 20.00

Unknown Manufacturer

Model:	Ryan New York – Paris
Year:	1930s
Wingspan:	3¼"
Price Range:	$20.00 – 40.00

Model:	Hughes's "Spruce Goose"
Year:	N.A.
Wingspan:	6"
Price Range:	$150.00 – 200.00

Model:	Douglas DC-3
Year:	1930s
Wingspan:	6"
Price Range:	$10.00 – 25.00

Model:	Aluminum biplane (N3N3)
Year:	1930s
Wingspan:	9"
Price Range:	$450.00 – 600.00

Model:	Aluminum biplane (0X-5)
Year:	1930s
Wingspan:	11½"
Price Range:	$450.00 – 600.00

Model:	Aluminum biplane (XYZ)
Year:	1930s
Wingspan:	12"
Price Range:	$450.00 – 600.00

Model:	Lockheed P-80
Year:	N.A.
Wingspan:	5"
Price Range:	$50.00 – 75.00

Model:	MIG-15
Year:	1980s
Wingspan:	3"
Price Range:	$10.00 – 20.00

Model:	MIG-21
Year:	1980s
Wingspan:	3"
Price Range:	$10.00 – 20.00

Model:	North Amer. F-86
Year:	1970s
Wingspan:	3¼"
Price Range:	$10.00 – 20.00

Model:	MIG-25
Year:	1980s
Wingspan:	3"
Price Range:	$10.00 – 20.00

Model:	Lockheed F-104
Year:	1970s
Wingspan:	2½"
Price Range:	$10.00 – 20.00

Model:	General Dynamics F-111
Year:	1970s
Wingspan:	3½"
Price Range:	$10.00 – 20.00

Model:	Lockheed SR-71
Year:	1980s
Wingspan:	2"
Price Range:	$10.00 – 15.00

Model:	Northrop F-5 "Freedom Fighter"
Year:	1980s
Wingspan:	2½"
Price Range:	$10.00 – 20.00

Model:	Douglas A4
Year:	1970s
Wingspan:	2"
Price Range:	$10.00 – 20.00

Model:	General Dynamics F-106
Year:	1970s
Wingspan:	2½"
Price Range:	$10.00 – 20.00

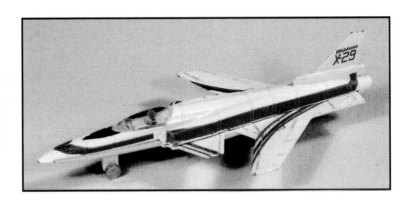

Model:	Grumman X-29
Year:	1980s
Wingspan:	2"
Price Range:	$10.00 – 15.00

Model:	North Amer. X-15
Year:	1980s
Wingspan:	2"
Price Range:	$10.00 – 15.00

Model:	Convair PBY "Catalina"
Year:	1970s
Wingspan:	4¾"
Price Range:	$10.00 – 20.00

Model:	Fairchild-Republic A10
Year:	1980s
Wingspan:	3¼"
Price Range:	$10.00 – 20.00

Model	Mitsubishi "Zero"
Year:	N.A.
Wingspan:	3¾"
Price Range:	$10.00 – 20.00

Model:	Sopwith triplane
Year:	N.A.
Wingspan:	4¾"
Price Range:	$10.00 – 20.00

Model:	Junkers JU-52
Year:	N.A.
Wingspan:	4½"
Price Range:	$10.00 – 20.00

Model:	Fokker E-I
Year:	N.A.
Wingspan:	3½"
Price Range:	$10.00 – 20.00

Model:	Junkers JU-88 "Stuka"
Year:	N.A.
Wingspan:	5"
Price Range:	$10.00 – 20.00

Model:	Racer
Year:	N.A.
Wingspan:	4"
Price Range:	$30.00 – 50.00

Model:	Wahl flying boat
Year:	N.A.
Wingspan:	4½"
Price Range:	$20.00 – 30.00

Model:	Feisler-Storch 156
Year:	N.A.
Wingspan:	4"
Price Range:	$10.00 – 20.00

Model:	Boeing #314 flying boat
Year:	N.A.
Wingspan:	5"
Price Range:	$20.00 – 30.00

Model:	Convair "Hustler" B-58
Year:	N.A.
Wingspan:	2½"
Price Range:	$10.00 – 20.00

Model:	Whistle plane
Year:	N.A.
Wingspan:	1¼"
Price Range:	$5.00 – 15.00

Model:	Toy pedal plane
Year:	N.A.
Wingspan:	2"
Price Range:	$10.00 – 20.00

Model:	Japanese monoplane
Year:	N.A.
Wingspan:	1½"
Price Range:	$10.00 – 20.00

Model:	Pierre biplane
Year:	N.A.
Wingspan:	½"
Price Range:	$20.00 – 30.00

This world's smallest biplane came from a dollhouse. How this plane was cast in this detail to show wheels, prop, and wing separation is unknown, but it is an interesting casting.

Model:	Thomas monoplane
Year:	N.A.
Wingspan:	½"
Price Range:	$5.00 – 10.00

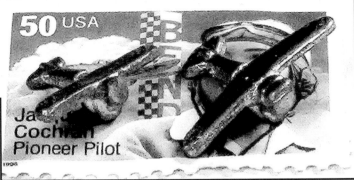

Model:	Henschel HS 123
Year:	N.A.
Wingspan:	3¾"
Price Range:	$10.00 – 20.00

Model:	Hawker "Seahawk"
Year:	N.A.
Wingspan:	4½"
Price Range:	$10.00 – 20.00

Model:	Biplane on floats
Year:	N.A.
Wingspan:	1¾"
Price Range:	$30.00 – 50.00

This sterling silver floatplane is a charming novelty, but not a charm.

Model:	B-2 bomber
Year:	N.A.
Wingspan:	5½"
Price Range:	$10.00 – 20.00

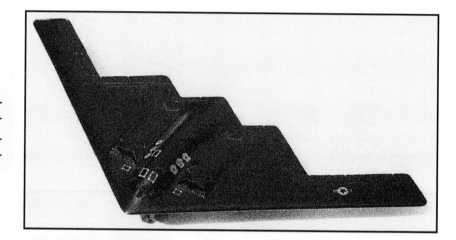

Model:	Red Baron Biplane
Year:	1991
Wingspan:	4¼"
Price Range:	$5.00 – 20.00

Model:	Douglas DC-3 (Lead)
Year:	N.A.
Wingspan:	3"
Price Range:	$10.00 – 20.00

Model:	B.A.C. – VC-10
Year:	N.A.
Wingspan:	3¼"
Price Range:	$10.00 – 20.00

Model:	P.Z.L. P11C
Year:	N.A.
Wingspan:	4¾"
Price Range:	$10.00 – 20.00

Model:	Royal Air Force SE-5
Year:	N.A.
Wingspan:	4"
Price Range:	$10.00 – 20.00

Model:	Mitsubishi "Zero"
Year:	N.A.
Wingspan:	3¾"
Price Range:	$10.00 – 20.00

Model:	Messerschmidt 410
Year:	N.A.
Wingspan:	3½"
Price Range:	$10.00 – 20.00

Model:	Messerschmidt 110
Year:	N.A.
Wingspan:	4"
Price Range:	$10.00 – 20.00

Model:	Fokker triplane DR.1
Year:	N.A.
Wingspan:	3¼"
Price Range:	$10.00 – 20.00

Model:	Biplane pencil sharpener
Year:	1980s
Wingspan:	3"
Price Range:	$2.00 – 5.00

Model:	Japan monoplane
Year:	N.A.
Wingspan:	1½"
Price Range:	$5.00 – 10.00

DIECAST TOYS

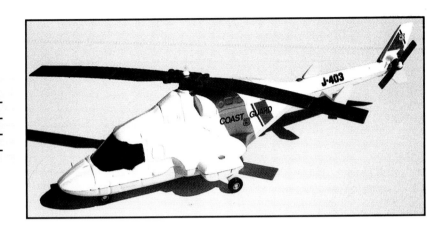

Model:	ERTL Bell 222B
Year:	1989
Length:	14"
Price Range:	$15.00 – 25.00

Model:	Dinky "Bristol" 173
Year:	1956
Length:	3½"
Price Range:	$75.00 – 100.00

Model:	ERTL "Apache" AH-64
Year:	N.A.
Length:	7"
Price Range:	$10.00 – 20.00

Model:	ERTL "Hind" MI 25
Year:	1988
Length:	7"
Price Range:	$10.00 – 20.00

Model:	ERTL "Hokum" KH28
Year:	1988
Length:	7"
Price Range:	$10.00 – 20.00

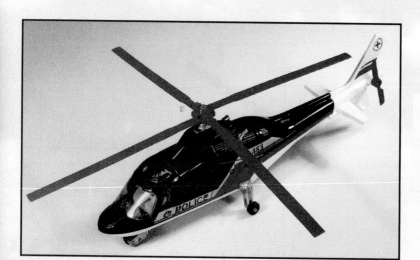

Model:	Majorette "Augusta" 109
Year:	N.A.
Length:	8½"
Price Range:	$15.00 – 25.00

Model:	Dinky Sikorsky S-58
Year:	1959
Length:	3"
Price Range:	$75.00 – 100.00

Model:	Corgi Bell "Iroquois" UHIN
Year:	1979
Length:	6"
Price Range:	$10.00 – 20.00

Model:	Dinky Bell "Trooper" 47
Year:	1973
Length:	6½"
Price Range:	$25.00 – 45.00

Model:	Dinky Sikorsky S-61 "Sea King"
Year:	1971
Length:	7"
Price Range:	$45.00 – 85.00

Model:	ERTL Bell "Iroquois" UH-18
Year:	N.A.
Length:	5½"
Price Range:	$10.00 – 20.00

Model:	Zee Sikorsky HH-3
Year:	N.A.
Length:	4"
Price Range:	$5.00 – 20.00

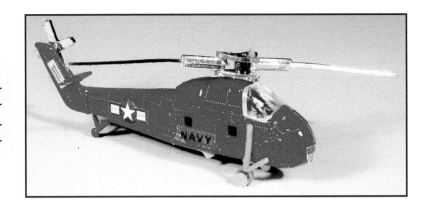

Model:	Zee Sikorsky S-58
Year:	N.A.
Length:	3½"
Price Range:	$5.00 – 20.00

Model:	Mercury Sikorsky S-55
Year:	N.A.
Length:	2½"
Price Range:	$25.00 – 40.00

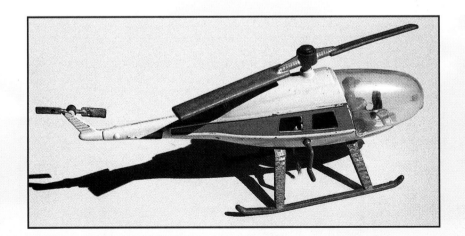

Model:	Gabriel Fairchild-Hiller FH-1100
Year:	N.A.
Length:	9"
Price Range:	$30.00 – 50.00

Model:	Hubley Piasecki "Mule" H-26A
Year:	1976
Length:	8"
Price Range:	$30.00 – 50.00

Model:	Solido Aerospatiale "Gazelle"
Year:	N.A.
Length:	7"
Price Range:	$15.00 – 20.00

Model:	Majorette Aerospatiale "Gazelle"
Year:	N.A.
Length:	5½"
Price Range:	$10.00 – 20.00

Model:	ERTL "Airwolf"
Year:	N.A.
Length:	5"
Price Range:	$10.00 – 20.00

Model:	Tootsietoy Bell Jet "Ranger"
Year:	1979
Length:	6"
Price Range:	$25.00 – 50.00

Model:	Solido Sud "Alouette II"
Year:	N.A.
Length:	7"
Price Range:	$15.00 – 25.00

Model:	Pla Me La Cierva autogiro
Year:	N.A.
Length:	3¼"
Price Range:	$30.00 – 50.00

Model:	Matchbox Westland "Puma"
Year:	1976
Length:	4¼"
Price Range:	$10.00 – 20.00

Model:	N.A. Vertol CH-47 "Chinook"
Year:	N.A.
Length:	3½"
Price Range:	$10.00 – 20.00

Model:	N.A. Sikorsky S-19
Year:	N.A.
Length:	5"
Price Range:	$10.00 – 20.00

Model:	Tootsietoy, Hiller 12C
Year:	1968
Length:	2¾"
Price Range:	$10.00 – 20.00

Model:	N.A. Sikorsky S-64 "Skycrane"
Year:	N.A.
Length:	5"
Price Range:	$15.00 – 25.00

Model:	Corgi "Batcopter"
Year:	N.A.
Length:	4¾"
Price Range:	$20.00 – 35.00

Model:	Matchbox "Seasprite"
Year:	N.A.
Length:	3"
Price Range:	$10.00 – 20.00

Model:	ERTL Sikorsky S-55 (RNAF)
Year:	N.A.
Length:	5"
Price Range:	$10.00 – 25.00

PRESSED STEEL & OTHER MODELS

Pressed Steel

Pressed steel toy planes were introduced to the U.S. toy market in 1920. Kingsbury was one of the first to have a line of steel planes most of which were around 15 inches in length. These were soon followed by the products of Boycraft, Keystone, and Steelcraft. Most of the early toys were monoplanes, but soon various trimotor models appeared on the scene. Steelcraft brought out the Lockheed "Sirius" in 1933 after the Lindberghs had completed their survey of oceanic air routes for Pan Am airlines and used a "Sirius" for this long journey.

Marx and Wyandotte companies entered the market a bit later with a multiplicity of models such as steel airliners, military bombers, and other models of planes that were popular and identifiable at the time with real aircraft which had made notable flights. Wyandotte's Lockheed "Vega" was a popular toy as the Vega had been known for its speed, and its role in the "round the world flight" by Wiley Post in 1931. Marx built several airliners and bombers of steel, and the steel items proved their durability by the longevity of the toys even as they were played with as hard as any type of toy planes. Many young boys expected these planes to fly and they were tossed around with vigor. The steel toys seldom bent or broke with the hard landings. Many Wyandotte and Marx planes can be found at toy shows and in antique toy stores today.

Since 1990 another type of pressed steel toy plane has arrived on the scene. The toy bank airplanes built by ERTL, SpecCast, and Gearbox have brought many new steel models to the collector. Durable by reason of the steel material and nicely finished with great paint jobs, these beauties show promise for attractive collection displays, and also offer the bank feature as a tool for savings. As new models arrive, the collector has an incentive to add another model and hope that a limited production will enhance the value of each model for future profit-taking.

Model:	Steelcraft Lockheed "Sirius"
Year:	1930s
Wingspan:	24"
Price Range:	$1,500.00 – 1,800.00

One of the most desirable of the Steelcraft planes, this "Sirius" model of 1933 had an advanced look because of the nickel-plated engine cowling and "wheel pants" to enhance aerodynamic drag in flight.

Model:	Chinese biplane
Year:	N.A.
Wingspan:	4¼"
Price Range:	$50.00 – 100.00

This metal biplane is a "penny toy" item which apparently originated in Asia, due to the costume and hat of the pilot.

Model:	Spec Cast North Amer. P-51
Year:	1995
Wingspan:	10"
Price Range:	$30.00 – 50.00

Model:	Spec Cast Travelair "Mystery S" racer
Year:	1992
Wingspan:	11"
Price Range:	$150.00 – 175.00

Model:	Spec Cast Stearman trainer
Year:	1992
Wingspan:	11"
Price Range:	$30.00 – 60.00

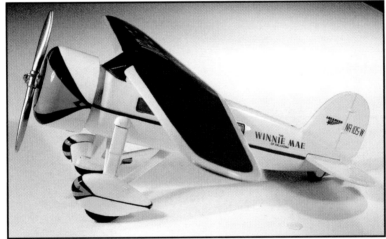

Model:	Spec Cast Lockheed Vega "Winnie Mae"
Year:	1992
Wingspan:	11"
Price Range:	$35.00 – 50.00

Model:	Spec Cast Beech 17 "Staggerwing"
Year:	1996
Wingspan:	11"
Price Range:	$30.00 – 45.00

Model:	ERTL Grumman "Widgeon"
Year:	1996
Wingspan:	12"
Price Range:	$30.00 – 45.00

Model:	ERTL Lockheed "Air Express"
Year:	1993
Wingspan:	12"
Price Range:	$30.00 – 60.00

Model:	ERTL Stearman 4E
Year:	1990s
Wingspan:	12"
Price Range:	$30.00 – 45.00

Model:	ERTL Northrop "Gamma"
Year:	1994
Wingspan:	13"
Price Range:	$35.00 – 50.00

Model:	Arch Pepsi Cola biplane
Year:	1990s
Wingspan:	8"
Price Range:	$30.00 – 50.00

Model:	Gearbox Stinson "Detroiter"
Year:	1990s
Wingspan:	12"
Price Range:	$50.00 – 75.00

Model:	Gearbox deHavilland DH-4
Year:	1990s
Wingspan:	11"
Price Range:	$50.00 – 75.00

Model:	Wyandotte Lockheed "Vega"
Year:	1930s
Wingspan:	18"
Price Range:	$150.00 – 400.00

Tinplate

This form of construction uses a more flexible form of metal which can be bent to shape. The brands which have been prominent in the market for a number of years include the Meccano planes and the many forms of Japanese tin planes which abound in Japan and the U.S.A. Of the latter, there must be more than 100 different models available with always some showing up at toy shows. These airliners range from 24" or more in wingspan and priced at more than $1,000.00 to smaller models at only several hundred dollars.

The Meccano planes are a heavier sheet metal than the Japanese tin planes, and some of these are assembled much like Erector sets with the use of nuts and bolts. The Meccano planes have become fairly rare in the United States in recent years, as most date back to the early 1930s and were an import from Great Britain.

Model:	Meccano "Tiger Moth"
Year:	1930s
Wingspan:	11"
Price Range:	$300.00 – 500.00

This toy plane is equipped with tin floats and wheels which are easily installed whenever desired.

Model:	Meccano biplane
Year:	1930s
Wingspan:	12"
Price Range:	$250.00 – 400.00

Model:	Builder trimotor
Year:	1988
Wingspan:	4"
Price Range:	$20.00 – 30.00

Model:	Builder monoplane
Year:	1990s
Wingsspan:	1½"
Price Range:	$10.00 – 20.00

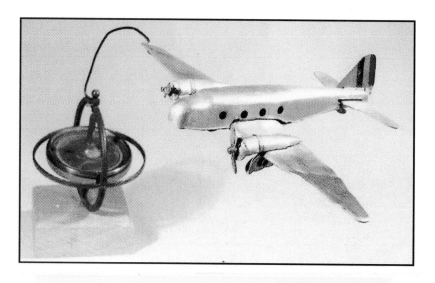

Model:	Twin-engine plane on a Gyro (France)
Year:	N.A.
Wingspan:	8"
Price Range:	$250.00 – 500.00

Model:	Crackerjack tin monoplane
Year:	1930s
Length:	2½"
Price Range:	$10.00 – 75.00

Model:	Tin floatplane
Year:	1980s
Wingspan:	4"
Price Range:	$20.00 – 30.00

Model:	Tin airliner
Year:	N.A.
Wingspan:	12"
Price Range:	$100.00 – 150.00

Model:	Tin DC-9 type jet airliner
Year:	1980s
Wingspan:	24"
Price Range:	$175.00 – 250.00

Model:	Ryan NY-P (lighter)
Year:	1980s
Wingspan:	7"
Price Range:	$125.00 – 150.00

Model:	Spad XII
Year::	1980s
Wingspan:	8"
Price Range:	$100.00 – 150.00

Plastic/Resin Formed Models

Model:	Antonov AN124 jet transport (Russia)
Year:	1980s
Wingspan:	15"
Price Range:	$150.00 – 200.00

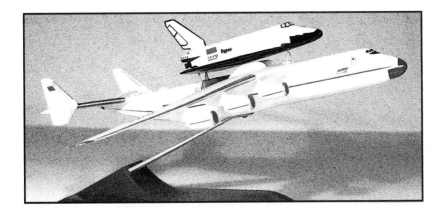

Model:	Antonov AN 225 jet transport w/Soviet shuttle
Year:	1989
Wingspan:	15"
Price Range:	$200.00 – 250.00

Model:	Antonov An225 transport (Russia)
Year:	1990
Wingspan:	24"
Price Range:	$450.00 – 600.00 (w/wood case)

Model:	Grumman "Gulfstream I"
Year:	1963
Wingspan:	13"
Price Range:	$90.00 – 150.00

Model:	Space Shuttle "Columbia" radio
Year:	1980s
Wingspan:	9½"
Price Range:	$100.00 – 150.00

Model:	Bachman Boeing P-26
Year:	1975
Wingspan:	2½"
Price Range:	$10.00 – 15.00

Model:	Bachman Curtiss P6E
Year:	1975
Wingspan:	2½"
Price Range:	$10.00 – 15.00

Model:	Gee Bee "R"
Year:	1970s
Wingspan:	6"
Price Range:	$10.00 – 20.00

Paper Models

Model:	Douglas DC-10
Year:	1999
Wingspan:	28"
Price Range:	$50.00 – 75.00

Fabric Models

Model:	U.S. Navy N3N3
Year:	1994
Wingspan:	22"
Price Range:	$75.00 – 125.00

Metal Desk Models/Presentation Models

Model:	Boeing SST
Year:	1982
Wingspan:	7½"
Price Range:	$200.00 – 300.00

Model:	Douglas A-20
Year:	1960s
Wingspan:	7½"
Price Range:	$75.00 – 125.00

Model:	deHavilland "Comet I"
Year:	N.A.
Wingspan:	9"
Price Range:	$200.00 – 350.00

Model:	Wiley Post Lamp
Year:	N.A.
Height:	19"
Price Range:	$250.00 – 450.00

Comic Character Models

Model:	Aviva toy "Snoopy & Sopwith Camel"
Year:	1978
Wingspan:	4½"
Price Range:	$40.00 – 80.00

Model:	United "Snoopy biplane"
Year:	1965
Wingspan:	3"
Price Range:	$20.00 – 40.00

Model:	Polisil (Italy) "Aero di Paperino"
Year:	N.A.
Wingspan:	4"
Price Range:	$40.00 – 60.00

Model:	ERTL "Whats up Doc?"
Year:	1988
Wingspan:	3"
Price Range:	$20.00 – 30.00

Model:	Deco Pac "Mickey Mouse" monoplane
Year:	N.A.
Wingspan:	5"
Price Range:	$20.00 – 40.00

Model:	ERTL "Aero Smurf" monoplane
Year:	N.A.
Wingspan:	3"
Price Range:	$20.00 – 30.00

Model:	"Bears biplane"
Year:	N.A.
Wingspan:	1½"
Price Range:	$10.00 – 15.00

Model:	"Bears light twin"
Year:	N.A.
Wingspan:	2"
Price Range:	$15.00 – 20.00

Model:	"Mr. Moon's homebuilt"
Year:	N.A.
Wingspan:	2"
Price Range:	$10.00 – 15.00

Model:	"Bear's racer"
Year:	N.A.
Wingspan:	1½"
Price Range:	$10.00 – 15.00

Model:	Corgi "Olive Oyl monoplane"
Year:	N.A.
Wingspan:	1½"
Price Range:	$15.00 – 20.00

Model:	"Chipmunk monoplane"
Year:	N.A.
Wingspan:	2"
Price Range:	$10.00 – 20.00

Space Models

Model:	Dinky "Trident Starfighter"
Year:	1979
Wingspan:	5½"
Price Range:	$50.00 – 90.00

Model:	Dinky "Eagle Transporter"
Year:	1975
Length:	8"
Price Range:	$50.00 – 90.00

Model:	Tootsietoy "Flash Gordon Ming"
Year	1978
Length:	5¼"
Price Range:	$25.00 – 40.00

Model:	PPC "USS Enterprise"
Year:	N.A.
Length:	6"
Price Range:	$10.00 – 25.00

Model:	Corgi NASA Space Shuttle
Year:	1980s
Wingspan:	4½"
Price Range:	$20.00 – 35.00

Model:	Dinky "Thunderbird"
Year:	1974
Length:	5½"
Price Range:	$50.00 – 90.00

Model:	Dinky "UFO Interceptor"
Year:	1971
Length:	6"
Price Range:	$50.00 – 90.00

Model:	Dinky "Klingon Battle Cruiser"
Year:	1979
Length:	7"
Price Range:	$50.00 – 90.00

Model:	Zygon "Maurader"
Year:	1979
Length:	8"
Price Range:	$50.00 – 90.00

Model:	ERTL "Batwing"
Year:	1989
Length:	5¾"
Price Range:	$15.00 – 25.00

Model:	Dinky "Zygon Patroller"
Year:	1979
Wingspan:	8½"
Price Range:	$50.00 – 90.00

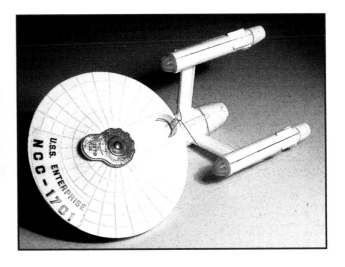

Model:	Dinky "USS Enterprise"
Year:	1976
Length:	9½"
Price Range:	$50.00 – 90.00

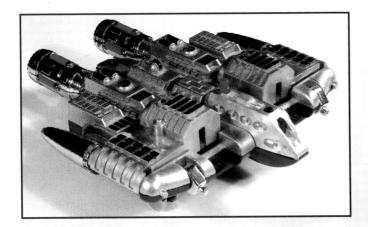

Model:	TOEI Space Ship (Japan)
Year:	N.A.
Length:	4"
Price Range:	$15.00 – 30.00

COLLECTING TOY PLANES TODAY

There are some essential things to know if one plans to start a collection or extend a collection in today's marketplace. The market is a bit different than it was even ten years ago. To search for toy planes the collector has many more venues to choose from, and the search methods now are not merely those of attending local toy shows and visiting toy stores. The toy shows that are significant are those that have national appeal and are attended by toy collectors from all over the country. Some of the major shows include: Chicago; Atlantic City; Glendale, California; San Francisco; Rochester, New York; several cities in Pennsylvania; and shows held in various locations throughout the Midwest.

The best way to identify the locations of shows that may be of interest to the collector is to subscribe to the *Antique Toy World, Toy Shop,* and other collector magazines. These publications will not only advertise the upcoming shows, but they also offer items for sale and a background on general toy collecting. It has been found that the history of toy manufacturers and their product lines gives the collector clues to specific toys and the prices they bring at different shows and auctions. Also, the publications' advertisements disclose the major toy shows that are scheduled and permit the collector an opportunity to plan a visit to shows in advance of the show date.

The various toy auction houses advertise in the toy publications and list their addresses and phones so the collector may make direct contact. Many of the auctions sell illustrated catalogs which identify and describe the items up for sale. They also provide for auction participation through phone-in or write-in bids, and offer notification of the auction results.

Toy shows are now held in all hub cities and many smaller cities, with the local newspapers advertising the date and time of shows that will accommodate collectors from a fairly large market area. The size of the show will depend upon how past history has benefitted dealers in sales volume. Some shows attract toy dealers who travel extensively and attend toy shows on a multi-state, or even national basis. This situation offers the dealer items from a large market area and offers choice pieces to collectors even in smaller communities.

Over the last few years it has been possible to search for toys on the Internet, a new technique for finding collectibles. One can sit at home and investigate the market for available toys and explore the inventory of many dealers with no actual footwork required. This method has the ability to tap into various sources and find unusual items. A credit card and computer are the only tools necessary.

Once you have started your collection, appraise the value of it, and if you have invested heavily, check with your insurer to see if your homeowner's policy would cover your loss if an item was stolen or otherwise lost. If your homeowner's policy will not cover your collection, consider an art/collectibles policy to provide reimbursement for loss. These policys are reasonably priced and do save the collector from considerable worry.

Note that while only a very few of the manufacturers listed in this volume are still producing toy airplanes, that new manufacturers have arrived on the scene in the last several years. A recent trip to a large hobby shop and a visit to a local air museum gift store produced a number of new miniature aircraft models not seen before. Many of these were diecast metal models and showed a high degree of detail.

Equipped with the information you now have, you are ready to begin your search for a collection of toy planes. Good hunting!

BIBLIOGRAPHY

Doucette, Joseph and C.L. Collins. *Collecting Antique Toys*. Macmillan, Publishing Co., 1981.

Foley, Dan. *Toys through the Ages*. Chilton Books, 1962.

Gardiner, Gordon and Alistair Morris. *Metal Toys*. Harmony Books, 1984.

Marchand, Frederic, Ed. *Avions-Jouets-Tome I*. Paris, France: Arte Adrien Maeght, 1993.

Stephan, Elizabeth, Ed. *O'Brien's Collecting Toys*. Krause Publications, 2001.

ABOUT THE AUTHOR

The first time aloft in 1931 in a Stinson "Detroiter" impressed the author with flying and from then on he was involved with airplanes. His military service during World War II was in Italy, and after completing his education at the University of Iowa and University of Washington he followed a vocation in aviation electronics. He worked with airlines, the military, and business aviation dealers and pilots. This provided a varied experience in aviation. Later, teaching college level classes in aero careers, the author also managed a consulting firm he founded. During retirement, he wrote for collectible magazines and published a CD "Parade in the Skies," a pictorial history of over 700 aircraft from 1903 to 2000, from his photos taken over fifty years. As a toy plane collector from 1970 on, the author has assembled this collection of toy planes with the help of collector friends who assisted with photos of

their special toys. Now he plans to resume wood and stone sculpture projects that were deferred and hike the trails in the forests and mountains of Washington State. The author is a member of the Antique Toy Collectors of America; the Antique Aircraft Association (Blakesberg, Iowa); The Museum of Flight (Seattle, Washington); and the Planes of Fame air museum (Chino, California).

Wishing all of you happy landings — and enjoy your "search"!

COLLECTOR BOOKS
informing today's collector

www.collectorbooks.com

For over two decades we have been keeping collectors informed on trends and values in all fields of antiques and collectibles.

6226	**Fostoria** Value Guide, Long/Seate	$19.95
5899	**Glass & Ceramic Baskets**, White	$19.95
6460	**Glass Animals**, Second Edition, Spencer	$24.95
6127	The **Glass Candlestick** Book, Vol. 1, Akro Agate to Fenton, Felt/Stoer	$24.95
6228	The **Glass Candlestick** Book, Vol. 2, Fostoria to Jefferson, Felt/Stoer	$24.95
6461	The **Glass Candlestick** Book, Vol. 3, Kanawha to Wright, Felt/Stoer	$29.95
6329	**Glass Tumblers**, 1860s to 1920s, Bredehoft	$29.95
4644	**Imperial Carnival Glass**, Burns	$18.95
5827	**Kitchen Glassware** of the Depression Years, 6th Ed., Florence	$24.95
5600	Much More Early American **Pattern Glass**, Metz	$17.95
6133	**Mt. Washington Art Glass**, Sisk	$49.95
6136	Pocket Guide to **Depression Glass** & More, 13th Ed., Florence	$12.95
6448	Standard Ency. of **Carnival Glass**, 9th Ed., Edwards/Carwile	$29.95
6449	Standard **Carnival Glass** Price Guide, 14th Ed., Edwards/Carwile	$9.95
6035	Standard Ency. of **Opalescent Glass**, 4th Ed., Edwards/Carwile	$24.95
6241	Treasures of **Very Rare Depression Glass**, Florence	$39.95

POTTERY

4929	**American Art Pottery**, Sigafoose	$24.95
1312	**Blue & White Stoneware**, McNerney	$9.95
4851	Collectible **Cups & Saucers**, Harran	$18.95
6326	Collectible **Cups & Saucers**, Book III, Harran	$24.95
6344	Collectible **Vernon Kilns**, 2nd Edition, Nelson	$29.95
6331	Collecting **Head Vases**, Barron	$24.95
1373	Collector's Ency. of **American Dinnerware**, Cunningham	$24.95
4931	Collector's Ency. of **Bauer Pottery**, Chipman	$24.95
5034	Collector's Ency. of **California Pottery**, 2nd Ed., Chipman	$24.95
3723	Collector's Ency. of **Cookie Jars**, Book II, Roerig	$24.95
4939	Collector's Ency. of **Cookie Jars**, Book III, Roerig	$24.95
5748	Collector's Ency. of **Fiesta**, 9th Ed., Huxford	$24.95
3961	Collector's Ency. of **Early Noritake**, Alden	$24.95
3812	Collector's Ency. of **Flow Blue China**, 2nd Ed., Gaston	$24.95
3431	Collector's Ency. of **Homer Laughlin China**, Jasper	$24.95
1276	Collector's Ency. of **Hull Pottery**, Roberts	$19.95
5609	Collector's Ency. of **Limoges Porcelain**, 3rd Ed., Gaston	$29.95
2334	Collector's Ency. of **Majolica Pottery**, Katz-Marks	$19.95
1358	Collector's Ency. of **McCoy Pottery**, Huxford	$19.95
5677	Collector's Ency. of **Niloak**, 2nd Edition, Gifford	$29.95
5564	Collector's Ency. of **Pickard China**, Reed	$29.95
5679	Collector's Ency. of **Red Wing Art Pottery**, Dollen	$24.95
5618	Collector's Ency. of **Rosemeade Pottery**, Dommel	$24.95
5841	Collector's Ency. of **Roseville Pottery**, Revised, Huxford/Nickel	$24.95
5842	Collector's Ency. of **Roseville Pottery**, 2nd Series, Huxford/Nickel	$24.95
5917	Collector's Ency. of **Russel Wright**, 3rd Editon, Kerr	$29.95
5921	Collector's Ency. of **Stangl Artware**, Lamps, and Birds, Runge	$29.95
3314	Collector's Ency. of **Van Briggle Art Pottery**, Sasicki	$24.95
5680	Collector's Guide to **Feather Edge Ware**, McAllister	$19.95
6124	Collector's Guide to **Made in Japan Ceramics**, Book IV, White	$24.95
1425	**Cookie Jars**, Westfall	$9.95
3440	**Cookie Jars**, Book II, Westfall	$19.95
6316	Decorative **American Pottery & Whiteware**, Wilby	$29.95
5909	**Dresden Porcelain** Studios, Harran	$29.95
5918	Florence's Big Book of **Salt & Pepper Shakers**	$24.95
6320	Gaston's **Blue Willow**, 3rd Edition	$19.95
2379	Lehner's Ency. of **U.S. Marks** on Pottery, Porcelain & China	$24.95
4722	**McCoy Pottery**, Collector's Reference & Value Guide, Hanson/Nissen	$19.95
5913	**McCoy Pottery**, Volume III, Hanson & Nissen	$24.95
6333	**McCoy Pottery Wall Pockets** & Decorations, Nissen	$24.95
6135	**North Carolina Art Pottery**, 1900 – 1960, James/Leftwich	$24.95
6335	Pictorial Guide to **Pottery & Porcelain Marks**, Lage	$29.95

5691	**Post86 Fiesta**, Identification & Value Guide, Racheter	$19.95
1670	**Red Wing Collectibles**, DePasquale	$9.95
1440	**Red Wing Stoneware**, DePasquale	$9.95
6037	**Rookwood Pottery**, Nicholson & Thomas	$24.95
6236	**Rookwood Pottery**, 10 Yrs. of Auction Results, 1990 – 2002, Treadway	$39.95
1632	**Salt & Pepper Shakers**, Guarnaccia	$9.95
5091	**Salt & Pepper Shakers** II, Guarnaccia	$18.95
3443	**Salt & Pepper Shakers** IV, Guarnaccia	$18.95
3738	**Shawnee Pottery**, Mangus	$24.95
4629	Turn of the Century **American Dinnerware**, 1880s–1920s, Jasper	$24.95
5924	**Zanesville Stoneware** Company, Rans, Ralston & Russell	$24.95

OTHER COLLECTIBLES

5916	Advertising **Paperweights**, Holiner & Kammerman	$24.95
5838	Advertising **Thermometers**, Merritt	$16.95
5898	Antique & Contemporary **Advertising Memorabilia**, Summers	$24.95
5814	Antique **Brass & Copper** Collectibles, Gaston	$24.95
1880	Antique **Iron**, McNerney	$9.95
3872	Antique **Tins**, Dodge	$24.95
4845	Antique **Typewriters & Office Collectibles**, Rehr	$19.95
5607	Antiquing and Collecting on the **Internet**, Parry	$12.95
1128	**Bottle** Pricing Guide, 3rd Ed., Cleveland	$7.95
6345	**Business & Tax Guide** for Antiques & Collectibles, Kelly	$14.95
6225	Captain John's **Fishing Tackle** Price Guide, Kolbeck/Lewis	$19.95
3718	Collectible **Aluminum**, Grist	$16.95
6342	Collectible **Soda Pop** Memorabilia, Summers	$24.95
5060	Collectible **Souvenir Spoons**, Bednersh	$19.95
5676	Collectible **Souvenir Spoons**, Book II, Bednersh	$29.95
5666	Collector's Ency. of **Granite Ware**, Book 2, Greguire	$29.95
5836	Collector's Guide to **Antique Radios**, 5th Ed., Bunis	$19.95
3966	Collector's Guide to **Inkwells**, Identification & Values, Badders	$18.95
4947	Collector's Guide to **Inkwells**, Book II, Badders	$19.95
5681	Collector's Guide to **Lunchboxes**, White	$19.95
4864	Collector's Guide to **Wallace Nutting Pictures**, Ivankovich	$18.95
5683	**Fishing Lure** Collectibles, Vol. 1, Murphy/Edmisten	$29.95
6328	**Flea Market Trader**, 14th Ed., Huxford	$12.95
6227	**Garage Sale** & Flea Market Annual, 11th Edition, Huxford	$19.95
4945	**G-Men and FBI Toys** and Collectibles, Whitworth	$18.95
3819	**General Store** Collectibles, Wilson	$24.95
5912	The **Heddon** Legacy, A Century of Classic **Lures**, Roberts & Pavey	$29.95
2216	**Kitchen Antiques**, 1790–1940, McNerney	$14.95
5991	**Lighting Devices** & Accessories of the 17th – 19th Centuries, Hamper	$9.95
5686	**Lighting Fixtures** of the Depression Era, Book I, Thomas	$24.95
4950	The **Lone Ranger**, Collector's Reference & Value Guide, Felbinger	$18.95
6028	Modern **Fishing Lure** Collectibles, Vol. 1, Lewis	$24.95
6131	Modern **Fishing Lure** Collectibles, Vol. 2, Lewis	$24.95
6322	Pictorial Guide to **Christmas Ornaments** & Collectibles, Johnson	$29.95
2026	**Railroad** Collectibles, 4th Ed., Baker	$14.95
5619	**Roy Rogers and Dale Evans** Toys & Memorabilia, Coyle	$24.95
6339	**Schroeder's Antiques** Price Guide, 22nd Edition	$14.95
5007	**Silverplated Flatware**, Revised 4th Edition, Hagan	$18.95
6239	**Star Wars** Super Collector's Wish Book, 2nd Ed., Carlton	$29.95
6139	Summers' Guide to **Coca-Cola**, 4th Ed.	$24.95
6324	Summers' Pocket Guide to **Coca-Cola**, 4th Ed.	$12.95
3977	Value Guide to **Gas Station Memorabilia**, Summers & Priddy	$24.95
4877	Vintage **Bar Ware**, Visakay	$24.95
5925	The Vintage Era of **Golf Club Collectibles**, John	$29.95
6010	The Vintage Era of **Golf Club Collectibles** Collector's **Log**, John	$9.95
6036	Vintage **Quilts**, Aug, Newman & Roy	$24.95
4935	The W.F. Cody **Buffalo Bill** Collector's Guide with Values	$24.95

This is only a partial listing of the books on antiques that are available from Collector Books. All books are well illustrated and contain current values. Most of these books are available from your local bookseller, antique dealer, or public library. If you are unable to locate certain titles in your area, you may order by mail from **COLLECTOR BOOKS**, P.O. Box 3009, Paducah, KY 42002-3009. Customers with Visa, Master Card, or Discover may phone in orders from 7:00a.m. to 5:00 p.m. CT, Monday – Friday, toll free **1-800-626-5420**, or online at **www.collectorbooks.com**. Add $3.00 for postage for the first book ordered and 50¢ for each additional book. Include item number, title, and price when ordering. Allow 14 to 21 days for delivery.

1-800-626-5420   Fax: 1-270-898-8890

www.collectorbooks.com

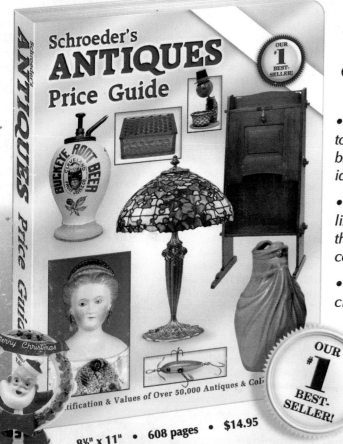